EVERYDAY DIALOGUES IN
ENGLISH

ROBERT J. DIXSON

EVERYDAY DIALOGUES IN

ENGLISH

A NEW REVISED EDITION

PRENTICE HALL REGENTS, Englewood Cliffs, New Jersey 07632

©1983 by Prentice Hall Regents
Prentice-Hall, Inc.
A Paramount Communications Company
Englewood Cliffs, New Jersey 07632

All rights reserved. No part of this book may be
reproduced, in any form or by any means,
without permission in writing from the publisher.

Printed in the United States of America

10

ISBN 0-13-292848-5 01

Prentice-Hall International (UK) Limited, *London*
Prentice-Hall of Australia Pty. Limited, *Sydney*
Prentice-Hall Canada Inc., *Toronto*
Prentice-Hall Hispanoamericana, S.A., *Mexico*
Prentice-Hall of India Private Limited, *New Delhi*
Prentice-Hall of Japan, Inc., *Tokyo*
Simon & Schuster Asia Pte. Ltd., *Singapore*
Editora Prentice-Hall do Brasil, Ltda., *Rio de Janeiro*

Cover design: Paul Gamarello
Text design: Judy Allan, The Designing Woman
Photo Editor: Robert Sietsema

We wish to thank the following for providing us with photographs:

Chase Manhattan Bank
New York Post Office
United States Department of Agriculture
The Southland Corporation
Metropolitan Transportation Authority
Gulf Photo Library
Kansas City Royals
Western Electric Photographic Services
Library of Congress
Atari Incorporated
The Sheraton Corporation
Hickey-Freeman Company
Wendy's International
Dentsply International
Columbia University
American Cancer Society
Ford Motor Company
United Nations
BMW of North America
National Center for Atmospheric Research/National Science Foundation
Sears Roebuck
Florida Department of Commerce/Division of Tourism

Preface

These dialogues cover a wide range of everyday situations, from buying groceries to flying in an airplane. Their vocabulary is that of everyday speech, and the expressions and idiomatic constructions are those heard wherever American English is spoken.

The purpose of the book is to acquaint those learning English with the vocabulary and particular forms of address used in these various situations. For example, how does one order a meal in a restaurant? What is the procedure to be followed conversationally when buying tickets for the theater or shopping for clothes? What are the common expressions to be used in making a telephone call? These are some of the things the book teaches, and naturally they are of importance to anyone learning English. The book should be useful to all students who wish to perfect their colloquial and idiomatic English. It should also be valuable for those who feel the need for additional vocabulary and further practice with idiomatic forms.

The book can also serve as a travel guide for those visiting the United States as tourists. Since most of the situations met in the course of one's everyday experiences are covered in the book, the visitor can find the necessary vocabulary and expressions with which to make himself or herself understood by people in all walks of life.

The book is also designed as an advanced conversation text. Since the dialogue form is used throughout, conversational forms are naturally stressed. In addition, adequate drill and study exercises accompany each of the dialogues. Questions follow each dialogue and provide a basis for further conversation between student and teacher. The teacher should naturally expand upon these questions and ask additional questions of a similar sort.

Teachers should also modify questions so that they apply appropriately to their particular students. One way to do this is to alter the wording of a question so that it is asked directly of a student. Teachers should also pay close attention to the vocabulary and the idioms used in these dialogues. They should make sure that the students understand all colloquial usage, whether it is included in the Vocabulary Practice exercises or not. Teachers should try to stimulate normal conversations which revolve around the essential vocabulary of the unit.

Contents

EVERYDAY DIALOGUES IN
ENGLISH

unit ① Opening a Bank Account

Chase Manhattan Bank/William R. Devin

CLERK: Good morning. May I help you?

MRS. OLSON: Yes. My husband and I have just moved here from Florida. We're just down the street, and you seem to be the closest bank. I'd like to open an account.

CLERK: Well, we're not only the closest bank, but we're also the most modern and convenient bank in the whole metropolitan area. Let me take you to our new accounts manager, Ms. Green. *(He leads her to a desk near the window.)* You sit here and as soon as Ms. Green is off the phone, she'll be glad to help you.

MS. GREEN: Good morning. I'm Edna Green. What may I do for you today?

MRS. OLSON: I'm here to open an account for my husband and myself. My name is Gretchen Olson.

MS. GREEN: Do you want a joint account, Mrs. Olson?

MRS. OLSON: Yes, we've always had a joint account. Tell me about your checking account policy. Is there a minimum balance required?

MS. GREEN: Yes and no. There is no minimum deposit required, but if you open your account with five hundred dollars or more and keep at least that much in it at all times, then there is no service charge. Also, we now pay interest on your checking account, so there's no need to keep a separate savings account.

MRS. OLSON: I'm not sure I understand about the five-hundred-dollar part. Could you explain that to me again, please.

MS. GREEN: Of course. Accounts are charged a monthly service charge of five dollars if the minimum balance in them falls below five hundred dollars at any time during the statement period. You may keep as little as three dollars in your account, but if you do, then we charge you five dollars at the end of the month since it went below the five-hundred-dollar minimum.

MRS. OLSON: I see. Now, since we'll be writing checks throughout the month, our balance will vary from day to day. How will you know what amount to use to figure our interest? I'd also like to know how much interest you pay.

MS. GREEN: The rate varies. Right now, it's six percent. It has gone as low as four and a half percent and as high as seven percent. Our computer adds all the daily figures and then divides by the number of days in your statement period. That's called your average daily balance. We use the average daily balance to figure the interest you've earned and credit it automatically to your account. The interest is printed on your monthly statement so you'll know to add it into your checkbook yourself. All bank charges and credits are recorded on your monthly statement.

MRS. OLSON: If you mean that five-dollar service charge, I can tell you that I'm going to try to avoid that charge. We should be able to keep more than five hundred dollars in our account all the time.

MS. GREEN: Yes, that's one type of bank charge, but there are others. The checks you'll be ordering today are an example. We'll decide what kind of checks you want and then charge your account for them. It will appear on your first month's statement. Of course, if a check of yours should be returned for insufficient funds, there would be a charge for that too.

MRS. OLSON: Do you mean bouncing a check? Unfortunately, I once had that experience. For a time both my husband and I were careless about recording the checks we had written. We overdrew our account twice and our checks bounced. Needless to say, we were embarrassed. We're much more careful these days.

MS. GREEN: You'd be surprised at how many people forget to record the checks they write. As you said, it's often a matter of carelessness; no one would bounce a check on purpose. Speaking of checks, why don't we look at the various styles available.

MRS. OLSON: *(She chooses her checks and completes several forms.)* I'd like to open this account with a deposit of one thousand dollars. Will it be all right if I write a check on our old account?

MS. GREEN: Certainly, as long as the account in your former bank is still active. By the way, since you are opening your account with one thousand dollars, you may choose one of the gifts which are displayed on that table over there. The bank is having a promotion to attract new customers. It's our way of welcoming you and thanking you for your business.

MRS. OLSON: Thank you. I like that travel alarm clock. Thank you for all your help. I'll ask my husband to come by here this afternoon so that he can sign the forms too. That way we'll both be able to start writing checks on our new account. How long will it take for the printed checks which I just ordered to arrive?

MS. GREEN: About ten days. Here, I want you to take one of our pamphlets which describes all our services.

MRS. OLSON: Thank you very much.

COMPREHENSION AND CONVERSATION PRACTICE

1. Where does this dialogue take place? What people take part in the dialogue?
2. Why did Mrs. Olson choose this particular bank?
3. What is the bank's minimum balance policy?
4. What does *bouncing a check* mean? What happens when a check bounces?
5. Why did Ms. Green offer Mrs. Olson a gift? Which gift did she choose?
6. What is a *joint* account? What other kinds are there?
7. What is the difference between a checking account and a savings account?
8. What are the duties of a teller in a bank?
9. What are the advantages of paying for purchases by check rather than in cash?
10. What are *traveler's* checks? How are they used?
11. Since this bank pays its customers interest for keeping their money there, how does it make a profit?

12. What is the procedure for taking out a loan?
13. What interest does your bank pay to its customers? What interest does it charge its customers who have taken out a loan?
14. What are *blank* checks? How are they useful?
15. What are some of the services offered by banks in your area? What are their hours?

VOCABULARY PRACTICE

1. A synonym for *certainly* is (maybe, of course, frequently, perhaps).
2. To *figure* interest on an account is to (deposit it, withdraw it, calculate it mathematically, draw it).
3. In banking terms, the opposite of a *charge* is a (saving, credit, statement, debit).
4. Which of the following words may be used as both a noun and a verb without any change in form? (withdraw, issue, receive, reimburse, continue, assume)
5. To *reimburse* is to (feel weak, open an account, pay back, repeat).
6. To *record* a check is to (film it, write it into a register, mail it, file it).
7. To be *active* is the opposite of to be (open, delinquent, closed, insufficient) in banking terms.
8. There's no *need* means there is no (necessity, fun, charge, trouble, bother).
9. To *write* a check is to make (over, for, in, out) a check.
10. A *pamphlet* is a (news bulletin, large book, booklet, magazine article).

Use Each of These Phrases in a Sentence
to cash a check • to open an account • at all times • of course • on several occasions • needless to say • as long as

New York Post Office

Mailing a Package at the Post Office

CUSTOMER: I'd like to mail this package to Brazil. How much will it be, please?

CLERK: Do you want to send it first class or parcel post?

CUSTOMER: How much is first class and how long does it take?

CLERK: It's a light package. *(He weighs the package.)* First class would cost $3.96. Since it's going to a large city, I would guess that it will take about four or five days to arrive.

CUSTOMER: And parcel post?

CLERK: Sending it parcel post would be cheaper, but it wouldn't arrive for about three weeks. The rate for parcel post is $2.05.

CUSTOMER: Oh, I want it to arrive earlier than that. I'll send it first class. Also, I'd like to insure it for $25.00.

CLERK: *(He fills out a form.)* What's in the package? I need to know in order to complete this form.

CUSTOMER: A pair of small glass earrings. They're a gift for my sister who's living in Rio. I packed them well, so I'm sure they won't break, but I want to insure them just in case.

CLERK: Do you want the package registered too? That way you would know that your sister received them. She would have to sign for the package, and then we would send you a receipt showing that your gift had been delivered.

CUSTOMER: No, I'm sure she'll let me know as soon as they arrive. Are there any other forms I need to fill out because it's going to a foreign country?

CLERK: Yes, one more. It's a customs declaration on which you declare what item or items are in the package and their value.

CUSTOMER: I understand that your rates have gone up on all postal items. Is that true?

CLERK: Yes, unfortunately, it is. The rates never seem to go down, do they? Here is a copy of all our new rates. It lists the old rate next to the new, so you can see how much it has gone up. Notice, however, that the rate for sending a postcard has remained the same.

CUSTOMER: I think I read something about the size of postcards and envelopes. Would you explain that to me, please?

CLERK: We used to accept postcards and envelopes of all

sizes, but now that we are using automatic sorting and postmarking machines, we have to limit the size. You can still send a letter in a large envelope, but it can't be any smaller than three and a half inches by five inches. Incidentally, you forgot to put a return address on this package. It's not a post office regulation, but we strongly recommend that all cards, letters, and packages have a legible return address.

CUSTOMER: I'll do it right now. I don't remember my zip code. Can you tell by looking at this address what it is?

CLERK: (He types the address into a small desk-top computer terminal.) Here it is. Your zip code is 22031. You should make a note of it.

CUSTOMER: I will. Before I leave, I want to buy some first-class stamps. Do you sell them in little packets?

CLERK: Yes. This one has twenty first-class stamps. Let's see. The package, the insurance, and the stamps. Your total bill is $9.12.

CUSTOMER: One more question. I expect to be out of town next week. Can you hold my mail for me here? I could come by to pick it up when I get back.

CLERK: Yes, we do that. You'd have to fill out one of these forms. You might also consider asking a neighbor to pick up your mail for you. It would be easier on you and on the letter carrier who sorts all the mail on your route.

CUSTOMER: Thanks. I'll think it over and let you know.

COMPREHENSION AND CONVERSATION PRACTICE

1. Where does this dialogue take place? What people take part in the dialogue?
2. What does the customer want to do?
3. What did the customer decide about sending the package? About the insurance? About the return receipt registry?
4. What is the post office regulation regarding the size of cards and envelopes?
5. What is a *zip code*? Why does the post office urge that everyone use zip codes?
6. What is the difference between *first-class* mail and parcel post? What is *second-class* mail? *Third-class* mail?
7. Why did the customer have to fill out a customs declaration?
8. How much does it cost to send a first-class letter? A postcard?
9. Why is it always advisable to put a return address on a letter or package?
10. What should a person do in order to have mail forwarded to a new address?
11. What happens when a letter carrier tries to deliver a registered letter or package, but there is no one at home?
12. How often is mail delivered? What are the normal hours that a post office is open?
13. How does a postal clerk determine how much to charge for a package being mailed?
14. What are some post office regulations regarding the wrapping of packages?
15. How long does it take, approximately, for a letter to go from your home to New York? To California? To Paris?

VOCABULARY PRACTICE

1. To *weigh* something, one usually uses a (meter, stamping machine, scale, stamp).
2. *Foreign* is the opposite of (modern, domestic, exaggerated, alien).
3. If a postal rate *goes down*, it (decreases, increases, stays the same, ends).

4. A *receipt* is a (direction for cooking, written acknowledgment, lie, money).
5. Another way to say *fill out* is (leave, fatten, complete, send).
6. A *postmark* is an official mark that (cancels, replaces, removes, erases) the stamp on a letter, card, or package and records the date and place of mailing.
7. In a *pound* there are (10, 12, 16, 20) ounces.
8. I'm *sure* means I'm (safe, okay, better, certain).
9. If you *pick* something *up* at the post office, you (retrieve it, leave it, lift it, improve it).
10. What are the verb forms of these nouns? (declaration, receipt, arrival, insurance, delivery, explanation)

Use Each of These Phrases in a Sentence

strongly recommend • can you tell • to make a note • let's see • I'll let you know

unit ③

United States Department of Agriculture.

Shopping at a Supermarket

CLARA: Hi, Mr. Plank. Will you help me for a minute, please?

MR. PLANK: Sure, Clara. How are you today? I haven't seen your mother or father in a while. Are they sick?

CLARA: Yes, as a matter of fact, they aren't feeling well. That's why I'm here to do some grocery shopping. They're not up to it, and we're almost out of food.

MR. PLANK: Well, I'll do anything I can to help. What do you need?

CLARA: I think I know my way around the store, but I'm not tall enough to reach some of the things on high shelves. Also, I'm not very good at deciding which fruits and vegetables are ripe and which ones aren't. I guess that's all, except for getting home. Do you think I could borrow one of the shopping carts when I'm finished? I'd bring it right back after I pushed the groceries home.

MR. PLANK: We'll find a way to get you home so you don't have to cross streets pushing that basket, Clara. Don't worry about that. Now, why don't you do all the shopping you can do alone. When you want me to reach for a high item, I'll help you. Save the fresh produce for last. When the time comes, we'll ask Mr. Sanchez to help you. He's the produce manager. Even though I'm the manager of the whole store, the individual department managers know more about their areas than I do.

CLARA: I'm a little nervous about choosing meat too.

MR. PLANK: If you need any help at the meat counter, just ring the bell for the butcher. Mrs. Athens is back there, and she'll be glad to help you.

CLARA: Thank you, Mr. Plank. My mother said she was sure you'd be kind and help me. I've never done this alone before. *(She consults her list and starts pushing her cart up and down the aisles. She finds most of what is on the list with no difficulty.)*

MR. PLANK: Well, how are you doing, Clara? Are you ready for my long reach yet?

CLARA: Actually, I'm doing pretty well. I've found almost everything, and it's been within reach. Would you help me decide about coffee? My list says "a pound of coffee," but it doesn't say what kind. All I know is that it has to work in an automatic coffee maker.

MR. PLANK: This brand is on sale this week, but you'll notice that this other can is cheaper even though it's not on sale. It's called a generic brand; that is, there is no fancy label, and they never advertise, so they can keep the price down. Some people prefer a brand they know, but others say these new generic brands are equally good. Why not try it this one time?

CLARA: Okay, Mr. Plank, I will.

MR. PLANK: I notice you have two quarts of skim milk. It's more expensive to buy milk that way, you know.

CLARA: No, I didn't.

MR. PLANK: If you buy your half gallon in a half-gallon plastic bottle, you'll save twenty to thirty cents.

CLARA: Gosh, thanks. I guess I have a lot to learn about grocery shopping. What do you think of this package of hot dogs that I picked?

MR. PLANK: You did very well there, Clara. That's the best buy in the prepared meats cooler. The price per pound is lower than any other brand, and they taste good. Will you want any hot dog buns to go along with the wieners? I know that's not on your list, but perhaps your mother forgot.

CLARA: It was my father who made the list. Maybe he did forget. Where are they? I'll get them, and if we don't need them now, then I'll freeze them.

MR. PLANK: Good thinking! I'll tell you what. You look around and see if there's anything else that you think your family needs, even if it's not on the list. Put it in your basket and pay for it at the checkout counter. Then when you get home, if your parents say they wish you hadn't bought something, just bring it back. I'll give you a full refund. After all, you're here doing the shopping, so you should be allowed to make some independent decisions about what you need. And don't forget to ask Mr. Sanchez for help when you get to the other side of the store.

CLARA: Thanks for all your help, Mr. Plank.

COMPREHENSION AND CONVERSATION PRACTICE

1. Where does this dialogue take place? What people take part in the dialogue?
2. Why is Clara shopping alone?
3. How old do you think she is?
4. What does she need help with? How does the store manager offer to help?
5. What is a *generic* brand? What advantages do generic brands have over more highly advertised brands? What disadvantages?
6. Why is it cheaper to buy larger quantity containers?
7. What is *drip* coffee? *Percolated* coffee? *Automatic drip* coffee?
8. Do you shop in a large chain supermarket? How do you like it?
9. What are the advantages and disadvantages of shopping in large chain stores?
10. What is *skim* milk? How is it different from other kinds of milk?
11. Describe what happens at a checkout counter.
12. What departments are there in a large supermarket?
13. How can you determine what the price per pound of an item is?
14. What does your family's normal weekly food shopping list have on it?
15. Where do Mr. Sanchez and Mrs. Athens work?

VOCABULARY PRACTICE

1. What is the full form of the following contractions? (I'm, aren't, I'd, we'll, I've, it's, you're)
2. *Incidentally* means (of course, by the way, certainly, pleasantly).
3. A *gallon* has (2, 4, 6, 8) quarts or (16, 32, 64, 128) ounces.

4. An example of *fresh produce* is (canned beans, frozen spinach, eggs, limes).
5. A *butcher* would deal with all of these except one: chicken, veal, bread, steak.
6. *Even though* means (in spite of, because, since, without).
7. The opposite of *expensive* is (costly, dear, small, cheap).
8. To *be good at* something is to (excel, leap, smile, look) at it.
9. A container that chills something and keeps it cold is called a (chiller, colder, cooler, keeper).
10. The adjective form of the noun *independence* is (independable, independing, independuous, independent).

Use Each of These Phrases in a Sentence

full refund • on sale • to learn about • the best buy • as a matter of fact • tall enough • right back • don't worry

unit 4

United States Department of Agriculture

Shopping for Fruit

CLARA: Excuse me. Are you Mr. Sanchez?

MR. SANCHEZ: That's right. And who might you be, miss?

CLARA: I'm Clara Savitz. Mr. Plank said I should ask you to help me. You see, I'm doing the shopping for my family this week because my mother and father are sick. I've done most of the shopping already, and now I want to get the vegetables and fruits on my list. My problem is that I don't know how to pick ripe ones. Will you help me?

MR. SANCHEZ: I'd be delighted. Let's see that list. Two pounds of sweet potatoes and five pounds of regular potatoes; let's start with these. First, we'll pull a plastic bag off this roll of bags. Notice how the bags are attached to each other at a place where the plastic is perforated? The way to separate them is to tear along this perforated line. *(He rips a bag from the roll.)*

CLARA: I'm glad you're helping me. I'm not tall enough to reach that roll. How do you know how many potatoes to put into the bag so that the bag will weigh five pounds?

MR. SANCHEZ: We'll start by putting in about eight or ten of these medium-sized Idaho potatoes. After you've done this for a while, you know how much things weigh even before you put them on the scale. Let's see how much these weigh. *(He puts the bag with nine potatoes in it on the scale.)*

CLARA: It says that we've got a little more than four pounds.

MR. SANCHEZ: Right. Now, let's leave the bag on the scale and add a few more potatoes one at a time. After adding each one, look at the arrow to see what the new weight is. When it points to somewhere near the five-pound mark, we'll stop. Here, you try it.

CLARA: It's just over five pounds now. Is that okay or should I take one back out?

MR. SANCHEZ: I think that's fine. You did well, Clara. Now I have to carry out a few crates of lettuce, so why don't you take these bags and do what we just did with the onions, apples, and green beans on your list. You won't have any trouble with them because I just put them out and they all look good. Just be sure to watch the scale.

CLARA: *(She weighs ten pounds of Bermuda onions, five pounds of apples, and two pounds of green beans.)* This isn't as hard as I thought it would be. Maybe I'll try picking out the tomatoes myself, since Mr. Sanchez still seems to be busy. I wonder how to tell which ones are ripe?

MR. SANCHEZ: Well, Clara, I see you've finished about half your list. Those tomatoes that you've chosen, however, aren't ripe enough. Notice how a lot of these are still green? That means they need a few more days in the sun. Here. We'll put in a few ripe, red ones for use in the next day or so, and we'll put in a few green ones. Those you'll put on the windowsill so they can ripen in the sunlight. That way you'll have fresh tomatoes later in the week.

CLARA: There's so much to learn! Here's another item I don't know much about. Bananas.

MR. SANCHEZ: Bananas are easy. Let's do it together. These aren't ripe enough to eat yet. You can tell because they're still green and hard. These are overripe; they're soft and black or brown-spotted. These yellow ones are firm and just right for eating. By the way, if you want to cook with bananas—bake banana bread, for example—then the black ones are fine, even better than the ripe ones.

CLARA: I feel as though I've learned a lot today. Now all I need is a half dozen oranges, and I'll be ready to take my cart to the checkout counter.

MR. SANCHEZ: I'm going off duty in about fifteen minutes, Clara. You should be through the line by then. Why don't you wait for me by the door, and I'll drive you home. Your packages would be too heavy to lift by yourself.

CLARA: Thanks, Mr. Sanchez. I'll do that. This has been quite an experience.

COMPREHENSION AND CONVERSATION PRACTICE

1. Where does this dialogue take place? What people take part in the dialogue?
2. What are the items on Clara's list? Which are fruits and which are vegetables?

3. Why did she need to weigh the potatoes, onions, apples, and beans?
4. How does a customer get a bag for fruits and vegetables?
5. Name some fruits with thick skins or peels. Name some with thin skins.
6. Oranges are called citrus fruits. What are some other citrus fruits?
7. What are some ways to cook potatoes?
8. Name some fruits which should be stored in the refrigerator and some which should not.
9. How did Mr. Sanchez teach Clara to weigh produce?
10. Do you have to weigh produce in your supermarket, or is it someone's job?
11. How can a person tell if a tomato is ripe?
12. How can a person tell if a banana is ripe?
13. Besides bananas, what fruits can one bake with?
14. What are your favorite vegetables?
15. How much fresh produce do you eat during a normal week?

VOCABULARY PRACTICE

1. The covering or skin of any fruit is generally referred to as the (heart, crust, top, peel).
2. When speaking of fruit, the opposite of *ripe* is (red, sour, juicy, green).
3. If you stepped on the peel of a banana, you would find it (hard, slippery, breakable, rough).
4. To *pick out* is to (criticize, refuse, choose, delay).
5. To be *delighted* is to be (enthusiastic, indifferent, bitter, angry).
6. Which of these words rhyme with *tear* in the sentence "Tear the bag along the perforated line"? (hear, near, dear, wear, bear, clear, fear, pear)
7. A *half dozen* means (3, 6, 12, 18).
8. When a person goes *off duty*, that person is about to (start working, stop working, work hard, get a promotion).
9. Five and one-quarter pounds is (5¼, 52½, 100, 84) ounces.
10. The opposite of *fresh* is (ripe, stale, new, modern).

Use Each of These Phrases in a Sentence

you see • I'd be delighted • let's see • it says • is that okay • just be sure • I wonder how • by the way • for example • even better.

Robert Sietsema

Going to the Theater

LYNNE: I hope we're not late, Anne. It's already 2:30.

ANNE: What time does the curtain go up?

LYNNE: It's supposed to start at 2:30 sharp, but I doubt it will. Even at these once-a-week matinees, the shows rarely begin on time. At least we're here. I was afraid I wasn't going to be able to get off work today.
(She speaks to the box office attendant.) I have two tickets for today's performance. Has the show begun?

ATTENDANT: Not yet, but you'd better hurry. Name, please.

LYNNE: Lynne Jefferson. I paid for the tickets by credit card over the phone about two weeks ago. I hope they're good seats.

ATTENDANT: *(He hands her the tickets.)* They're in the second balcony about halfway up, but they are on the aisle.

LYNNE: That's pretty high. I don't suppose you have anything better which we could exchange these for? Have there been any last-minute cancellations?

ATTENDANT: No, there's nothing left at all for today's show. In fact, we're sold out for three weeks in advance.

LYNNE: That's what they told me when I made these reservations. Oh, well, it's better than not being here at all, I suppose. *(Lynne and Anne enter the theater, hand their tickets to an usher, and then climb the stairs to the second balcony.)* I've been reading such good reviews of this play. I hope we're not disappointed.

ANNE: Me too. I've loved the leading lady in her movie roles for years. It'll be interesting to see if her talent can be transferred to the legitimate theater. *(The usher for the second balcony shows the women to their seats.)*

LYNNE: Here we are: Row M, seats 2 and 4. These are not so bad. What do you think?

ANNE: I think . . . oh, there go the house lights. The play's about to begin. We'd better get settled.

LYNNE: *(At the conclusion of Act I, the curtain closes and the house lights go on, signaling an intermission.)* Wow! That was pretty powerful acting! I didn't realize she was such a good actress. What did you think?

ANNE: I was impressed too. However, there was something about the supporting actor with the uniform. You know the one I mean—with the mustache.

There was just something wrong. . . .

LYNNE: I know what it was. I noticed it too. It's the makeup he's wearing. It's all wrong. He's supposed to be a fifty-year-old man, but he looks twenty-five.

ANNE: That's right, yes, of course. Oh, let's go to the lobby and mingle among the people. I love to see what theatergoers are wearing and eavesdrop on conversations.

LYNNE: Let's listen in so we can hear if other people agree with us about the play.

ANNE: How did you like the stage setting in that final scene of Act I? I see here in the program that the set was designed by a member of the cast. In fact, she's married to the actor I mentioned a minute ago —the one whose makeup is wrong. A married couple appearing in the same play. Imagine!

LYNNE: I liked the set of the musical comedy we saw last week better. Remember, they changed the scenery and props constantly. The variety attracted me more than this single set. I must admit that I get a little bored watching the same room for an entire act.

ANNE: Well, musicals naturally have more variety, but I don't like having the story interrupted by songs all the time. I prefer a serious drama such as this one.

LYNNE: Speaking of "this one," we'd better get back to our seats. I think Act II is about to begin. We can talk more at the next intermission.

ANNE: Good idea. I don't want to miss any of it.

COMPREHENSION AND CONVERSATION PRACTICE

1. Where does this dialogue take place? What people take part in the dialogue?
2. What time did their show begin? What time do evening shows usually begin?
3. Are ticket prices more or less expensive at a matinee performance?
4. How often do you go to the theater? What was the last play you saw?
5. Which do you enjoy more, a movie or a play? Why?
6. Why is it necessary to make reservations in advance for a stage play?
7. What is the difference between a musical comedy and a drama?
8. What is the difference between seats in the orchestra and seats in the balcony? Which are cheaper?
9. What did the two ushers in the dialogue do?
10. How do house lights signal the start of a play or an act in a play?
11. What did the women think of the first act? Of the actors?
12. Why did they want to go to the lobby?
13. What is a *set*? Who designed the set in the play the women were watching?
14. What did Anne think of the musical she saw last week?
15. What kind of a role would you like to play in a theater production?

VOCABULARY PRACTICE

1. A *matinee* is always presented (at night, in the afternoon, in the morning).
2. *Nothing left* means (nothing in addition, nothing to the left, nothing new, nothing remaining).
3. A person in a theater who directs you to your seat is called (a caddy, a porter, a waitress, an usher).
4. In the sentence, "It's the makeup he's wearing," *makeup* means (cosmetics, pretense, fabrication, construction).

5. The opposite of being *bored* is being (casual, drilled, designed, excited).
6. If a show is *sold out,* then tickets are (obtainable elsewhere, completely sold, partly sold, sold only by reservation).
7. Give the opposites of these terms: late, closes, wrong, agree, married, constant, serious.
8. A *member of the cast* is a person who works in the stage production as (a stagehand, a technician, an actor or actress, an usher, a box office attendant).
9. A *mustache* is something a man grows on his (upper lip, head, chin, arm).
10. Give the meaning for each of these theater terms: act, scene, prop, house lights, curtain, intermission, stage, leading lady, on the aisle.

Use Each of These Phrases in a Sentence

2:30 sharp • in your name • last-minute • at all • in fact • in advance • I suppose • to get settled • to get back • I see here • Imagine! • good idea • speaking of

unit 6

The Southland Corporation

Shopping at a Convenience Store

MRS. TURNER: Thanks for picking me up at work this evening, Ted. I really appreciate it.

TED: No problem, Mom. I'm happy to do it. By the way, I had some friends over after school today, and I'm afraid we drank all the milk in the fridge. Shall we stop at the supermarket on the way home to get some for tomorrow morning?

MRS. TURNER: I think the supermarket's closed by this time of night. But we can stop at the convenience store over on Highway 57. That's not too far out of our way, and I know they'll be open. They're open twenty-four hours a day.

TED: *(He drives to the store his mother mentioned.)* Here we are. You were right; the sign says "Open 24 hours." I don't think I've ever been here before. Let's go in.

MRS. TURNER: This place certainly is different from the huge store we're used to, isn't it, Ted? I don't come here often because I think the prices are higher than at a regular grocery store.

TED: It seems to be an easy store to find things in, though. And it also seems to have at least one of everything. There isn't much of a selection. I mean there are only one or two brands of each type of merchandise, but that makes choosing easier, doesn't it?

MRS. TURNER: Easier than what? I enjoy comparing brands so I can get the best bargain for our family. Usually I'm not in a hurry, so I have the time to compare and get the most for my money. Of course, this time we don't have much of a choice, do we?

TED: No, I guess not. This is probably the only place open at this time of night. If we want milk and ice cream, we'll have to buy them here.

MRS. TURNER: Ice cream too? Our list seems to be growing longer. Oh, well, I guess we can pick up some ice cream—if it's not too expensive. At least we don't have to wander around looking for the dairy products department. There's the ice cream freezer over there next to the milk and eggs.

TED: Actually, I'd like to get an ice cream cone, if it's okay with you. The packaged kind doesn't taste as good as the kind they put on cones. These days, most stores don't sell ice cream in cones.

MRS. TURNER: I guess that's another difference between these kinds of convenience stores and the larger supermarkets. They even serve ice cream cones here; you'd never see that in a larger place.

TED: Look at this, Mom. These are hamburgers and hot

dogs that are all ready to eat. They're wrapped in some sort of plastic. It says on the label that all you have to do is put the sandwich into the microwave oven for about thirty seconds, and it will be hot and ready to eat!

MRS. TURNER: If you're hungry, we'll make egg salad sandwiches when we get home. I'll pick up a dozen eggs here. That way we'll be sure to have enough. You'd better go over to the magazine rack and browse. It'll take your mind off food. I'll pay for the milk and eggs, and we'll be ready to go. *(She takes her groceries to the counter.)*

MR. KIM: Good evening, ma'am. I'm Mr. Kim, the new evening manager. Did you find everything you wanted?

MRS. TURNER: Yes, I did. Thank you. I'm surprised at your milk prices. They're much lower than I expected. Your store is not only convenient to shop in, but also your prices are competitive with the larger chains. How do you do it?

MR. KIM: The prices are low only on selected items. We can't really compete on all that we sell. But at least there are no long lines.

MRS. TURNER: Here you are, Mr. Kim. *(She hands him a ten-dollar bill.)* And please take out for two ice cream cones too. Okay, Ted, what kind of ice cream would you like?

COMPREHENSION AND CONVERSATION PRACTICE

1. Where does this dialogue take place? What people take part in this dialogue?
2. How old do you think Ted is?

3. Where is the convenience store in the dialogue? How late is it open?
4. What are the advantages of shopping in a convenience store? The disadvantages?
5. What is the difference between shopping at a convenience store and shopping at a large supermarket?
6. What did Ted and his mother buy at the store?
7. What are your favorite flavors of ice cream?
8. What are some advantages of microwave ovens? Some disadvantages?
9. How much does milk cost where you shop? How much are eggs?
10. Name some items which you probably cannot buy in a convenience store.
11. Name some items which you cannot buy in a regular grocery store.
12. What kinds of magazines are sold in convenience store racks?
13. How far do you have to drive to the nearest food store?
14. What do you think of the sandwiches that come wrapped in plastic?
15. Which type of store do you prefer to shop in?

VOCABULARY PRACTICE

1. Choose the correct tag ending for this sentence: "We haven't been here before, (do we, have we, haven't we, were we)?"
2. Frozen food, such as ice cream, is kept in a (cooler, icer, rack, freezer).
3. When a store is open *twenty-four hours*, it is open (every day, all day, all day and all night, three days a week).
4. To *browse* is to (shed, inspect leisurely, buy, read thoroughly).
5. The noun form of the verb *compete* is (competison, competity, competition, competability).
6. Another way to say *thirty seconds* is (half a minute, a minute, a few minutes, several minutes, a long time).
7. The word *though* rhymes with (through, rough, cough, bough, dough).
8. Which of the following items are *not* dairy products? (milk, butter, eggs, magazines, yogurt, hamburgers, cheese, cones)

9. Which of the following times is considered an evening hour? (7:00 a.m., 12:00 noon, 12:00 midnight, 7:00 p.m.)
10. A common synonym for the adjective *convenient* is (cheap, handy, selected, competitive).

Use Each of These Phrases in a Sentence

I'm afraid • by this time • out of our way • it seems • in a hurry • of course • I guess/I guess not • to pick up • to take out (money) • take your mind off • long lines

unit (7)

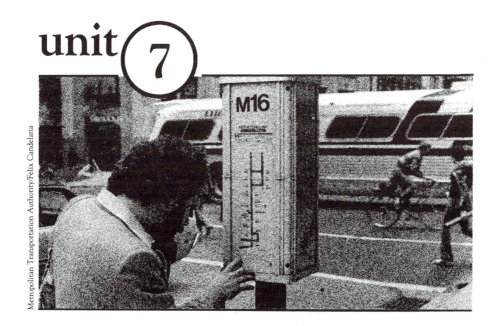

Metropolitan Transportation Authority/Felix Candelaria

Asking Directions

TOURIST: Excuse me, sir. I'm trying to find my way to the church that Frank Lloyd Wright designed. I forget the name of it, but I'm told that it's one of the most beautiful buildings in the city.

NATIVE: Yes, I know the one you mean. You must be new in town. We get a lot of tourists asking where that church is. Are you driving or taking public transportation?

TOURIST: Today I'm taking buses. You're right; I am a tourist. I drove here yesterday and spent the day driving to all the sights, but today I have decided to go by bus.

NATIVE: That's good. It's slower, but you'll get to see more of the city riding the bus. First of all, you're on the wrong street. You have to walk more than two blocks to Garvey Boulevard where you'll catch the

A-12 bus. Take it about a mile. When you pay the driver, be sure to ask for a transfer; you'll need it. Get off the A-12 at Prescott Avenue and transfer to the M-16 bus going north.

TOURIST: Maybe I should write all this down. I don't want to get lost. Let's see. That's the A-12 to Prescott, then transfer to the M-16 going north.

NATIVE: Right. Ask the last driver to let you off at Valley Road. The church you're looking for is only a short walk from there. You can't miss it.

TOURIST: Thanks. I appreciate your help.

SECOND NATIVE: Young man, I couldn't help but overhear your conversation with the gentleman who just gave you directions.

TOURIST: Yes, ma'am?

SECOND NATIVE: I think he must be confused, because the directions he gave you are all wrong. If you follow them, you'll have a lovely ride, but you'll end up at the zoo.

TOURIST: What should I do, then?

SECOND NATIVE: Walk with me. I'm heading in the direction where you'll be catching the bus you want. Where are you from? I don't recognize your accent.

TOURIST: I'm from Lima, Peru. That's in South America. This is my first visit to the States, and I want to see as many sights as I can.

SECOND NATIVE: I've never visited your country. The farthest south I've ever been is Mexico City. Well, here we are. This is the corner of Wall Drive and Utley Street, and here is your bus stop. Take the S-1, which will stop right where we're standing, down to the lake. The bus will turn right, but you should get off and cross the street. It's called Shore Lane.

TOURIST: And that's where the Frank Lloyd Wright church is?

SECOND NATIVE: No. You'll see another bus stop with a sign like this one. All the bus stops here have the same bright-colored signs, so they're easy to spot. Transfer there to the T-2 going south. The end of the line for the T-2 is just across the street from the Frank Lloyd Wright church. The whole ride shouldn't take you any more than thirty minutes.

TOURIST: Thank you. I'm glad you set me straight. It would be easy to get lost in a town this large.

SECOND NATIVE: It's not difficult to find your way around if you have a good map of the city. I recommend that you buy one. There's a definite plan to the way the city is designed and the streets are named. If you study a map, you'll find out how easy it is.

TOURIST: Is that my bus coming down the street now?

SECOND NATIVE: Yes, it is. I hope you have the correct change.

TOURIST: Why? Won't the driver make change for me?

SECOND NATIVE: Not any more. In the old days, drivers made change for people, but now you have to have the correct amount. When you get on, you drop the fare into a fare box which sits on the floor next to the driver. When you want to get off, pull the cord above the side windows to signal the driver.

TOURIST: At least that's the same. Our Peruvian buses also use the cord signal. I hope I don't get lost. Thank you and goodbye.

COMPREHENSION AND CONVERSATION PRACTICE

1. Where does this dialogue take place? What people take part in the dialogue?
2. Where does the young man want to go? Why?
3. Where did he come from? When? Why is he in that city?
4. What did the first person tell him to do?
5. What did the second person tell him?
6. Is the city in the dialogue near water? How do you know?
7. Could you give directions to a stranger in your city?
8. Which buses do you regularly ride?
9. Do you find that most people are able to give good directions?
10. Is it difficult to find your way around in your city?
11. What are the advantages and disadvantages of riding public transportation?
12. What is a *transfer?*
13. Are there any famous buildings near where you live? Which?
14. Besides the one mentioned in the dialogue, do you know any other famous architects?
15. What is a *zoo?*

VOCABULARY PRACTICE

1. Give the opposites of these words: south, west, wrong, above, difficult, left, last, lost.
2. If a person wants to *see the sights,* then that person is interested in (having a vision, visiting interesting places, buying glasses).
3. To *catch* a bus is to (get off it, miss it, park it, board it).
4. The cost of riding a bus is called a (fare, transfer, change, map).
5. If someone tells you, *"you can't miss it,"* then it is probably (impossible, hard, easy, crazy) to find it.
6. A *mile* is about (1, 1.6, 2, .6) kilometers.
7. Easy to *spot* means easy to (soil, draw on, see at a distance, buy).
8. Choose the correct preposition: I usually come to class (in, on, at, by) bus.

9. Another way to say *thirty minutes* is (a quarter of an hour, half an hour, an hour).
10. To *set someone straight* is to (turn them around, correct them, relax them, fire them).

Use Each of These Phrases in a Sentence

I'm told • first of all • to be sure • I couldn't help but • to end up • to set a person straight • to get lost • to find one's way around • to find out • in the old days • all wrong

unit (8)

Gulf Photo Library

Filling the Tank with Gas

MS. PORTER: Fill it up, please.

MR. KOBAK: You're at the self-service island, Ms. Porter. If you want me to fill your tank, you'll have to pull over to the lane marked "full service."

MS. PORTER: Oh, Mr. Kobak, I forgot. I pulled in here out of force of habit, I suppose. I usually fill the tank myself in order to save money. But today I'm dressed for a job interview, and I don't want to take the chance of getting my clothes dirty. I'll pull over to the full-service island.

MR. KOBAK: I know that your car takes unleaded gas, but I forget whether you buy regular or high-octane no-lead.

MS. PORTER: I usually get the regular, but perhaps I should try the high-test. What do you think? The car has been a bit sluggish lately.

MR. KOBAK: I think you should stick with the regular. Your car doesn't really need the higher octane, so it wouldn't pay for you to get the more expensive kind. Your car has been sluggish because it's been too long since your last tune-up. I remember when you left it here to be worked on. That was months ago.

MS. PORTER: Okay. I'll stick with the regular, and I'll bring the car in for some servicing in a week or so. Would you check the oil, please?

MR. KOBAK: *(The attendant checks the oil.)* It's just a little below the "full" mark. It won't take a whole quart. Perhaps you should let it go until you come in next week. We'll change your oil then and fill it up.

MS. PORTER: Good idea. While you're under the hood, would you mind checking the water in the radiator and in the battery? It's been ages since I last checked them.

MR. KOBAK: The radiator's all right, but this battery needs some water. You don't want to let this level get too low. Some morning you'll wake up and the car won't start. There. That should hold you for a while. Uh-oh. I forgot to check the temperature level in your radiator. I'd better do that now.

MS. PORTER: What do you mean "the temperature level"?

MR. KOBAK: Winter will be here in no time, so we have to be sure that your radiator water can withstand the freezing temperatures. This gauge I'm putting into the water will tell us how low the temperature can go before your water turns to ice. It's actually a measure of the amount of antifreeze left in your tank from last winter. It looks okay to me. It says that it would have to get down to fifteen below before you had a problem. It never gets that cold around here.

MS. PORTER: I hate to ask after all you've done, but do you think you could check the tires too? The front ones need twenty-nine pounds of pressure and the rear ones need thirty-two.

MR. KOBAK: *(The attendant fills the tires with air and finishes pumping the gas.)* I'll clean off this windshield now, and you'll be all set for your interview.

MS. PORTER: Do you know the best way for me to get to the interstate highway from here? I usually take the bus into the city and save my driving for these suburban roads, so I don't know my way around town too well.

MR. KOBAK: Sure thing, Ms. Porter. Turn left and go two blocks. Then turn right onto Sepulveda and go three-quarters of a mile. The entrance to the interstate is well marked. You can't miss it.

MS. PORTER: How much do I owe you?

MR. KOBAK: That'll be twenty dollars even. *(She hands him a twenty-dollar bill.)* Drive carefully, Ms. Porter, and don't forget to bring your car in next week.

COMPREHENSION AND CONVERSATION PRACTICE

1. Where does this dialogue take place? What people take part in the dialogue?
2. At a gas station, what is a *self-service* island? A *full-service* island?
3. What is the difference between leaded and unleaded gasoline? Which cars need which type?
4. What is the purpose of using a high-octane gasoline?
5. Besides filling the tank, what services did Mr. Kobak perform for Ms. Porter?
6. Why didn't she pump her own gas?
7. How do you know when your car needs oil?

8. Why do the radiator and the battery in a car need water?
9. Besides the radiator and the battery, what else is "under the hood"?
10. What is the job of antifreeze in a radiator?
11. Do you know what psi (pounds per square inch) of air your tires need?
12. What is a windshield wiper, and what does it do?
13. What is the difference between an interstate and a regular road?
14. How much does gasoline cost where you live?
15. How many miles (kilometers) does your car go on a gallon (liter) of gas?

VOCABULARY PRACTICE

1. The word *gauge* rhymes with (laugh, page, dig, hog, fridge).
2. If a motor is slow to respond, it could be described as (full, checked, sluggish, okay).
3. If it's been *ages,* then it's been (a long time, a short while, a few minutes, a reasonable amount of time).
4. When the attendant said, *"that should hold you,"* he meant that what he did was probably (not enough, too much, more than enough, sufficient).
5. *In no time* means (soon, much later, never, without time).
6. The opposite of being *all set* is being (prepared, rigid, solid, not ready).
7. *Twenty dollars even* means (around $20, exactly $20, a little less than $20, $20 and some change, a little more than $20).
8. The title *Ms.* is used to signify (a man, a woman, a single woman, a married woman).
9. The title *Mr.* is used to signify (a man, a woman, a single man, a married man).
10. At what temperature Fahrenheit does water turn to ice? (0°, 32°, 37°, 98.6°, 100°)

Use Each of These Phrases in a Sentence

to pull over • force of habit • to take a chance • to stick with • it wouldn't pay for you • let it go • it's been ages • wait a minute • in no time • to be all set • sure thing • don't forget

Robert Sietsema

Taking a Taxi

FIRST RIDER: Hello. Is this the Red, White, and Blue Taxi Service?

DISPATCHER: Yes, it is. You'll have to speak a little louder. We have a bad connection.

FIRST RIDER: I need a taxi, please. I'm taking a train today, and my bags are too heavy to carry on and off the bus.

DISPATCHER: What time do you need a cab, ma'am?

FIRST RIDER: My train leaves at 6:15, but I think I should arrive at the station no later than 5:30. How long is the ride from here?

DISPATCHER: From where? I don't know where you live.

FIRST RIDER: I'm sorry. I live at 435 Riverside Drive. And I have three medium-sized bags.

DISPATCHER: Let's see. Well, since it's rush hour, I'd say that the ride would take about thirty minutes, more or less. We should probably pick you up about 5:00. Is that okay?

FIRST RIDER: Yes, that will be fine. The driver will help me with my bags, won't he?

DISPATCHER: *She.* The driver is a she, ma'am, and yes, she'll help you with your bags.

FIRST RIDER: *(The doorbell rings at 4:55.)* Oh, I'm glad to see that you're here on time, miss. These are my bags. *(They put the bags into the taxi and then get in.)* How much is this going to cost me?

DRIVER: Watch the meter. My guess is that it'll cost you about five or six dollars, but if we get stuck in rush-hour traffic, it could go higher.

FIRST RIDER: I thought you used to charge by the number of zones you drove through.

DRIVER: We used to do it that way, but we changed to the meter system a few years ago. Has it been a long time since you took a taxi?

FIRST RIDER: More years than I care to remember. How long have you been driving?

DRIVER: I've been driving for about six years now. It's a good living. I get to meet interesting people; most weeks the business is good; I'm out in the air instead of behind a desk. There are a lot of reasons why I like it.

FIRST RIDER: Watch out for that truck!

DRIVER: How about letting me do the driving?

FIRST RIDER: I'm sorry. It looked as though that truck was going to hit us, and you are driving pretty fast. Are we in much of a hurry? Am I going to be late? Oh, dear, I'm so nervous driving in all this traffic. Why are we stopping?

DRIVER: *(She rolls down the window and speaks to a person on the sidewalk who has his hand raised to hail a taxi.)* Where are you headed?

SECOND RIDER: The train station. But you already have a passenger, don't you?

DRIVER: Yes, but there's room for you if it's all right with her. What do you say, ma'am? I know it's against the rules, but it's not out of our way, and it is getting cold out there. Do you mind if we take on an extra passenger?

FIRST RIDER: Not at all. That's kind of you. I hope you won't get into any trouble over this.

DRIVER: I hope not too. Get in. We're all going to the train station. Now try not to be so nervous. If I drive too cautiously, we'll never get you to your train on time. I have to take some chances once in a while. I'm a good driver; I haven't had an accident in six years with this company, so don't worry.

SECOND RIDER: I'm sure she knows what she's doing. The taxi drivers in this city are excellent drivers, and since the more fares they get the more money they make, it's fair to say that for them "time is money." That's why they have to drive fast.

FIRST RIDER: I'm not used to taking taxis, sir. *(In a whisper)* I wonder if you could advise me on an appropriate amount to tip our driver?

SECOND RIDER: Anywhere from ten to twenty percent of the total on the meter would be appropriate. It depends on how good a job you think she's doing, whether she's polite, whether she helps you with your bags, etc. I'm going to give her a good tip for stopping to pick me up. I was getting cold standing on that corner, and all the other taxis that passed refused to stop.

DRIVER: Here we are. Okay, the meter says $5.75. Let me help you with your bags. Sir, you got in about two-thirds of the way here, so let's say that your bill is $4.00. Is that fair?

COMPREHENSION AND CONVERSATION PRACTICE

1. Where does this dialogue take place? What people take part in the dialogue?
2. When did the first rider think the taxi was going to arrive at her home? What time did it actually arrive?
3. What time did her train leave? What time did she want to get to the station?
4. What is the purpose of a *meter* in a taxi?
5. What are the taxi rates in the city where you live?
6. When was your last taxi ride? Where did you go?
7. Are most taxi drivers courteous? Are most of them good drivers?
8. Why was the first rider nervous?
9. Why did the driver become exasperated with the first rider?
10. What does the expression *time is money* mean?
11. How much do you think you should tip a taxi driver?
12. Why do you think it was against the rules for the driver to pick up an extra passenger?
13. Do you think the driver picked up the man on the street corner to be kind, or did she want to make some extra money?
14. What is traffic like during the rush hour where you live?
15. What reasons did the driver in the dialogue give for enjoying her job?

VOCABULARY PRACTICE

1. Which of the following does not mean *no later than* 5:30? (5:15, 5:20, 5:30, 5:35)
2. When we want to know if someone approves, we ask (Where are you headed? What time is it? What do you say?)
3. What parts of speech (noun, verb, adjective) are these words? (fare, fair, cab, nervous, roll down, take on, says)
4. A *tip* given to a driver at the end of a ride is (advice, a push, a nod of the head, a small sum of money).
5. *Where are you headed?* means (Where are you? Where are you going? Where were you? Where will you sit?)
6. To *hail a taxi* is to (telephone one, sit in one, signal one by calling out or raising one's hand, take one).
7. Another word for *taxi* is (meter, truck, desk, cab).
8. *Two-thirds* of something is (25%, 33⅓%, 66⅔%, 75%) of it.
9. The expression *behind a desk* means (driving a taxi, working in an office, being out in the air, working at a train station).
10. A voice that *whispers* speaks (quietly, loudly, not at all, kindly).

Use Each of These Phrases in a Sentence

no later than • how long • on time • my guess is • to get stuck • to watch out • how about • what do you say • do you mind • not at all • to get in • it depends

unit (10)

Kansas City Royals

Watching a Baseball Game

PETER: It's good of you to take the trouble to accompany me to my first baseball game, George. We don't play baseball much in Europe, you know, but I've always wanted to see the game for myself. I've always wondered what it was about the sport that excites so many people.

GEORGE: It should be a good game today. The professional teams play one hundred sixty-two games each season from April through October. As this is the last week in September, you can see that the season is coming to an end. The two teams we're going to see tonight are tied for first place in the American League Western Division. They both want to make the playoffs, so they'll be playing their best. It should be an example of baseball as it should be played.

PETER: What are the names of the teams?

GEORGE: The California Angels and the Kansas City Royals.

PETER: What colorful names, and what colorful uniforms! I'm looking forward to this experience. I hope I can understand what's going on.

GEORGE: I'll do my best to explain. Let's start with the guy out there in the middle. He's called the pitcher. His job is to throw the ball to the catcher—the man behind the plate.

PETER: What about the man with the stick?

GEORGE: That's called a bat. The man with the bat tries to hit the ball before it gets to the catcher. If he misses the ball on three tries, he's "out." If three players are counted "out" like that, the other team gets to bat. Are you following me?

PETER: I think so. As soon as three players are out, then the other team gets its turn. But what happens if the batter hits the ball?

GEORGE: Good. If the batter hits the ball, the other team tries to catch it before he gets to a base. If one of the players catches the ball before it touches the ground, that's also counted as an "out." If they don't catch the ball, the batter runs to a base.

PETER: And there are four bases?

GEORGE: Right, four bases including the plate where the batter stands to hit the ball.

PETER: Is this how a player gets runs for his team?

GEORGE: Yes, that's right. If the batter, or runner, makes it all the way around the bases, his team gets a run. The team that gets the most runs wins the game.

PETER: I see that there are nine players in the field. You've told me the positions of two of them—the pitcher and the catcher. What are the other players called?

GEORGE: The player to the right of the pitcher standing near first base is called the first baseman. The one directly behind the pitcher is the second baseman, and the one over to the left is the third baseman. The man who is playing in between the second and third basemen is called the shortstop. The three guys playing far out in the grassy area are called outfielders.

PETER: Look! The batter just hit the ball a long way.

GEORGE: Yes, but it went foul.

PETER: Is that bad?

GEORGE: No, it's just than any ball which is hit outside of the limits of the playing field is foul. Ordinarily, it counts as a strike, unless the batter already has two strikes. Then it doesn't count, and the batter has another chance to hit the ball.

PETER: There! He's hit it again! That time it went on the ground to the one at third base, and he threw it to the first baseman before the batter ran there. What's happening?

GEORGE: He grounded out. That was the third out for that team, so the side is retired. That's the end of the first inning. There are nine innings in the game.

PETER: Who's the man in the dark blue outfit behind first base?

GEORGE: Oh, he's an umpire—like a referee in football. There are usually three or four of them working every game. They're the ones who decide whether

the pitcher has thrown a ball or a strike—I'll explain what they are later—and whether runners are
safe or out when they run the bases.

PETER: I think I'll stop asking questions for a while. I'm
getting a bit overloaded with all this information
and all these new terms. I'll just watch and enjoy
what I'm able to understand.

COMPREHENSION AND CONVERSATION PRACTICE

1. Where does this dialogue take place? What people take part in the dialogue?
2. Which teams are playing? What league are they in?
3. What is the job of the pitcher? The catcher? The batter?
4. What are the other positions on a baseball team?
5. What happens each inning?
6. What happens if nine innings are played and the score is tied?
7. What is a *foul ball?*
8. How many outs is each team allowed each inning?
9. How many players are there on a baseball team? A basketball team? A soccer team?
10. What is a *grounder?*
11. What is the function of an umpire in a baseball game?
12. How popular is baseball where you live?
13. Would you like to be a professional baseball player? What position would you like to play?
14. Can you name any famous baseball players? Who is your favorite baseball player?
15. Which teams played in the World Series last year?

VOCABULARY PRACTICE

1. In the phrase *to understand what's going on, going on* means (traveling, talking a lot, continuing, happening).
2. A baseball game is divided into nine (quarters, runs, innings, sets).

3. What preposition is used as penalty in baseball? (up, out, over, under, in)
4. The stick that baseball players use to hit the ball is called a (mallet, racquet, bat, mitt).
5. Another word for *umpire* is (referee, player, shortstop, batter).
6. The pitcher throws the ball past the batter to the (outfielder, first baseman, umpire, catcher).
7. An association of sports teams is called a (group, school, league, game).
8. Which of the following words rhymes with *foul?* (bowl, howl, soul, towel, vowel, pool)
9. Each team is allowed (1, 3, 9, 162) outs per inning.
10. *Are you following me?* in this dialogue means (Are you behind me? Do you understand me? Where are you? What do you want?)

Use Each of These Phrases in a Sentence

good of you • you know • to look forward to • to do one's best • that is • in between • doesn't count • what's happening • for myself

unit 11

Making a Phone Call

FRED: I'd like to speak to Donna Gregory, please. This is Fred Easter.

WRONG NUMBER: I'm sorry, but I think you must have the wrong number. There's no one here by that name. What number were you calling?

FRED: I was calling 555-2893. Maybe my finger slipped, and I touched the wrong button. I have one of those touch-tone phones.

WRONG NUMBER: No, you called the right number. That is, this is 555-2893, but there's no one named Gregory here.

FRED: Sorry to have bothered you. I'll check the number again. *(They both hang up. Fred dials the information number, 411.)*

OPERATOR: Information for what city, please?

FRED: Chicago. I'm trying to locate a Donna Gregory on Michigan Avenue.

Western Electric Photographic Services

OPERATOR:	Business or residence, sir?

FRED: It's a business.

OPERATOR: I have a Gregory Associates at 452 Michigan Avenue in Chicago. The number is 555-2983.

FRED: Darn! I transposed the middle numbers. Thank you. *(He hangs up and dials the correct number.)*

RECEPTIONIST: Gregory Associates. Good morning.

FRED: Good morning. I'd like to speak to Donna Gregory, please. This is Fred Easter.

RECEPTIONIST: I'm sorry, but Ms. Gregory is out of town until Friday. Is there anyone else who can help you?

FRED: No, I really need to talk to her. Is there a way I can reach her or at least leave a message for her to call me?

RECEPTIONIST: I can give you the number in San Francisco where she can be reached. It's 980-1375. The area code for San Francisco is 415. In case you don't reach her, Mr. Easter, why don't you leave your number with me. That way she'll have a message to call you when she gets back on Friday.

FRED: Thank you. That's very thoughtful. My number here in Chicago is 555-4002. Thanks for your help. I'll try the number you gave me. *(He hangs up and dials California.)*

CLERK: Hotel San Luis. May I help you?

FRED: Donna Gregory, please. I don't know the room number.

CLERK: I'll ring Ms. Gregory's room, sir. *(The phone rings ten times.)* I'm sorry, sir. No one seems to answer. Would you care to leave a message?

FRED: Yes. Please ask Ms. Gregory to call Fred Easter in Chicago. She knows the number. Tell her it's urgent that I speak with her, and that she should call no matter what time it is. I have call forwarding on my phone, so no matter where I am, her call will automatically be transferred to me.

CLERK: I'll tell her.

FRED: Oh, speaking of forwarding calls, does Ms. Gregory have one of those beepers? Do you know what I mean? There are a lot of commercial names for them. It's a device that people carry so they can be signaled when there is a message for them. I always just call it a beeper.

CLERK: Yes, sir, I know what you mean, but I don't know whether she has one or not. She didn't leave any word with us on how to contact her. All I can do is put a message in her box and activate the message light on her room phone. Will there be anything else, sir?

FRED: No, thank you. You've been very helpful. Goodbye.

COMPREHENSION AND CONVERSATION PRACTICE

1. Where does this dialogue take place?
2. How many people are involved in this dialogue? Who are they?
3. Why did Fred get a wrong number?
4. How do you answer a person who has called your phone by mistake?
5. When you get a wrong number, what do you say?
6. What number do you dial for information? Is there a charge for this service?

7. What number do you dial for a police or fire emergency? To find out the correct time? The weather?
8. How much does it cost to use a pay phone where you live?
9. How do you get your name and number listed in the phone directory?
10. What is an *area code*? What is your area code?
11. What is *call forwarding*? How is it useful?
12. How many phones are there in your home? What kinds are they?
13. What is a *person-to-person* call? How do you make one?
14. What are the usual phrases for starting and finishing a telephone conversation? What are some variations that you have heard?
15. What is your telephone number?

VOCABULARY PRACTICE

1. A *wrong* number is (a late, an ambiguous, a left, an incorrect) one.
2. To *bother* is to (amuse, cause annoyance, applaud, suspect).
3. If I want to *reach* you by phone, then I want to (get in touch, touch, stretch, dial).
4. When you finish talking on the phone, you hang it (on, down, to, up).
5. Which numbers in this sequence are *transposed*? (1, 2, 3, 4, 6, 5, 7, 8, 9, 10)
6. Something which requires immediate action is (unimportant, urgent, leisurely, wrong).
7. What are the opposites of these words? (wrong, helpful, anything, hang up, thoughtful, private, no one, incorrect)
8. Which of these phrases is not an appropriate way to answer a telephone? (Hello, Good morning, Goodbye, Good afternoon)
9. A partner or colleague in business may be called (a boss, an employee, a consultant, an associate).
10. If a device *beeps,* it (makes a noise, flashes a light, dials a telephone, activates a light, leaves a message).

Use Each of These Phrases in a Sentence

darn • I'm sorry • out of town • to check . . . again • to hang up •
to reach someone • to leave a message • to get back • would you
care to . . . • no matter what time

unit (12)

Library of Congress

Touring Washington, D.C.

KAREN: This is really exciting, Janet. Here we are in our nation's capital at last. I never thought I'd be able to save the money to go on this class trip.

JANET: Neither did I, Karen. Those after-school jobs your uncle got us were just what we needed. What's the first thing you want to see this morning?

KAREN: Let's go to the Capitol. Mr. Horst told our social studies class that you can go to your representative and ask for a pass to see Congress in session. That's what I'd like to do. Let's go to Rep. Hayden's office and ask for passes. My Mom and Dad voted for him, but I don't think they ever met him.

JANET: Maybe we should aim higher. Let's go to Senator Wolf's office and ask her for a pass to see the Senate in session. It might be more exciting than watching the House of Representatives.

KAREN: Sounds good to me, but the first thing we'd better

do is figure out how to get around by public transportation. The subway here is called the Metro. I hear that it's a pretty efficient way to get around the city.

JANET: *(The girls ride the subway but get off at the wrong stop.)* I don't think that building looks much like the Capitol. Let's go over and see what the sign says.

KAREN: *(She looks at her street map.)* I can tell you where we are. I just saw a sign for George Washington University. According to the map, we're miles from the Capitol.

JANET: What are we near?

KAREN: The State Department, the Lincoln Memorial, and the Kennedy Center for the Performing Arts are all within a five- or ten-minute walk. Want to see them while we're at this end of town?

JANET: Why not? *(They set off on foot.)* That's a really impressive statue of Abraham Lincoln. He was a great man. I think he's my favorite president.

KAREN: Mine is John Kennedy. He seems more real to me because so many members of his family are still active and in the news. Oh, look at that sight!

JANET: According to your map, this is called the Reflecting Pool. We're at one end of the Mall looking east. And that, of course, is the Washington Monument. Over there to the right is the Jefferson Memorial. Let's walk down the Mall.

KAREN: Look over there to the left. The green area is called the Ellipse and that building on the other side of it has the most famous address in the whole country.

JANET: Of course, 1600 Pennsylvania Avenue. The White

House. Do you think we can take a tour of it?

KAREN: Sure. I read in a guide back at our hotel that certain parts of the White House are open to the public all year. Let's see if we can join a tour.

JANET: *(An hour later)* That was a great tour. I'm disappointed that we didn't get to see the President or anybody famous, but it was fun to see such a famous building. Let's go back to the Mall and walk toward the Capitol.

KAREN: Let's stop and eat first. Look, over there is a sidewalk vendor. That looks like an interesting building he's standing in front of. We can sit on its steps and eat our lunch.

JANET: You're right; it is an interesting-looking place. It reminds me of a medieval castle. Look at the map. What is it?

KAREN: It's the original Smithsonian Institute building. I can't wait to tell my friends where I ate lunch today.

JANET: That lunch hit the spot. Shall we go to one of the museums? There's the Air and Space Museum. I hear that it's the most popular and the most visited public building in the United States.

KAREN: I'd love to see it, and I'm still interested in seeing the House or Senate in session, but I'm worn out. I haven't done this much walking in years. I suggest we take the Metro back to our hotel and take a nap. We can always come back here later.

COMPREHENSION AND CONVERSATION PRACTICE

1. Where does this dialogue take place? What people take part in the dialogue?
2. What is the difference between a capital and the Capitol?
3. What are the two houses of Congress called? What are the titles of the men and women who serve in these houses?
4. What is a *subway?* What is the subway in Washington called?
5. What do the letters *D.C.* stand for? Why are they used?
6. What famous places did the girls visit?
7. Which presidents did they say they admired most?
8. Where does the president live?
9. Who is the current president of the U.S.? How many others can you name?
10. Can you name any senators or representatives?
11. What do sidewalk vendors sell?
12. Why are there monuments to Washington, Jefferson, and Lincoln?
13. What would you most like to see if you could visit Washington, D.C.?
14. What topics are studied in a social studies class?
15. Who did you (or your parents) vote for in the last election?

VOCABULARY PRACTICE

1. If something *hits the spot,* it's (awful, enjoyable, invisible, a target).
2. To be *worn out* is to be (tired, rested, old, warm).
3. That which refers to the Middle Ages is called (new, middle, open, medieval).
4. Sleeping for a short time is called (snoring, dreaming, waking, napping).
5. If the House of Representatives is *in session,* then they are (at home, on vacation, in their offices, campaigning, meeting).
6. Visits to interesting places can be called (guides, tours, passes, plans).
7. What is called the Foreign Ministry in many countries is called

(the Kennedy Center, the Smithsonian Institute, the Mall, the State Department) in the United States.

8. *On foot* means (running, walking, riding, with shoes on).
9. Which of these words rhymes with *tour?* (sour, four, hour, poor, roar)
10. An expression which means the same as *sounds good to me* is (interesting music, good idea, it figures, I can hear you).

Use Each of These Phrases in a Sentence

at last • just what we need • to start with • sounds good to me • to figure out • to get around • to get off • looks like • to set off • on foot • all year • to come back

unit (13)

Atari Incorporated

Playing Video Games

RICKY: Come on, Aunt Sara. Try it. It's fun. After all, video games have been around for years. Millions of people play them all the time. We even have a couple that we play at home on our home computer.

AUNT SARA: I know, I know. It just seems so noisy in here. And there are so many people. I must admit that everyone looks happy. Your friends seem to enjoy all the excitement.

RICKY: It is a great place to meet my friends and to meet new people too, but there's also a lot of skill involved. Here, let me put some money in this old Space Invaders game. It's one of the earliest video games. It's practically a classic, and it's easy to understand and learn to play.

AUNT SARA: Why don't you play a game or two first, so I can see how to do it.

RICKY: No, it's best if you just jump in with both feet, so to speak. You probably won't do too well the first few times, so don't expect too much. Just try and, above all, concentrate on what you're doing.

AUNT SARA: I'm probably the oldest person in the entire arcade. Oh, what does it matter? I promised you I'd give it a try, so let's go. Put the money in, and we'll see how your old Aunt Sara zaps the invaders from space.

RICKY: This lever in the middle—we call it a joy stick—is how you move your gun across the bottom of the screen. The invaders will drop bombs, which are actually electronic impulses, at varying speeds from various places across the screen. Your job is to move your gun underneath them before the bombs hit the ground.

AUNT SARA: Do I shoot them?

RICKY: Yes, by pressing this button over here. If you hold it down, it fires continuously; otherwise, it only fires a burst when you depress it.

AUNT SARA: That's all there is to it?

RICKY: Well, not exactly. As the game progresses, the invaders come faster and faster and drop more bombs, so you have to move more rapidly and get the guns under them and blast them out of the sky. What was that word you used? "Zap" them. That's it. Okay, you're on your own. *(He puts coins in the slot.)*

AUNT SARA: Zap! Pow! Take that, you evil aliens! Oops, that one sneaked past me! Oh, no! He got me, Ricky. The little devil was too fast, but I'll get him next time. Here are a few dollars. Get some change, and we'll try again. Oh, this is fun!

RICKY: You're becoming a pro at this game, Aunt Sara. Your scores are getting higher and higher with each game that you play. Would you like to move on to a more complicated game?

AUNT SARA: Eventually, but for now I'd like to concentrate on getting the best score ever on this game.

RICKY: If you do that, Aunt Sara, you can enter your initials in the video display to show everyone that you got the highest score.

AUNT SARA: What a good idea. They never had anything like that on the pinball machines. That's what we used to play when I was your age. Why don't I come to your house tomorrow and try my hand at some of the games you have on your home computer. You could explain all the different types of games to me before we come back here to the arcade. Would that be all right?

RICKY: Aunt Sara, I think you're hooked.

COMPREHENSION AND CONVERSATION PRACTICE

1. Where does this dialogue take place? What people take part in the dialogue?
2. Why do people go to video game arcades?
3. What is the atmosphere like in one of these arcades?
4. What is the object of the Space Invaders video game?
5. How much does it cost to play one of these games in an arcade?
6. Which is your favorite video game?
7. What is a *pinball* machine?
8. What other types of games are popular at amusement centers?
9. How popular are amusement centers where you live?
10. Describe the noises made by video games. How do you spell such words?

11. Besides playing video games, what else can a person do with a home computer?
12. In computer language, what is a *program?*
13. How do home computers differ from large computers used in business?
14. Why might a person spend money to play a video game at an arcade when he or she could play the same game at home?
15. What does it mean to be *hooked?* Are there any games which you are hooked on?

VOCABULARY PRACTICE

1. *What does it matter?* means (it's very important, I'm too old, it's not important, I'm too young).
2. The opposite of *noisy* is (quiet, loud, still, happy).
3. *Video* is also used to refer to which of these? (radio, stereo, tape recorder, TV)
4. Another way to say *so to speak* is (speak up, talk louder, in other words, say it again).
5. To *give it a try* is to (give it up, lose it, attempt it, forget it).
6. If a person is addicted to or snared by a custom, then that person could be said to be (played, hooked, sneaked, fired).
7. Give the past tense form of each of these verbs: sneak, blast, hurt, seem, become, get, depress, progress.
8. The opposite of *continuous* is (continued, intermittent, perfect, crowded).
9. Which of the following words is *not* an acceptable adjectival form of the verb *vary?* (variable, varying, various, varied, variful)
10. An example of a *few* dollars is ($1, $3, $100, $1000).

Use Each of These Phrases in a Sentence
come on • all the time • to put in • to jump in with both feet • above all • give it a try • let's go • you're on your own • next time • to move on • try my hand at • to come back

unit 14

Jane Latta

Filling a Prescription

PHARMACIST: Good evening, Mr. Binns. What can I do for you tonight?

MR. BINNS: I have a long list of things we need, Mr. Kreck. Most of them I think I can find on your shelves without any help, but I do need you to fill this prescription for me, if you will.

PHARMACIST: Wait just a minute, and I'll see if I have this in stock. If I have to order it, it may take a day to fill, but if I have it in stock, I should be able to fill this in ten minutes or so.

MR. BINNS: I'll start picking up some of these items on my list while you look. Let's see, aspirin, a roll of adhesive tape, a bottle of vitamin C tablets. . . . I wonder what size I should get. *(He continues talking to himself while walking along the drug aisle.)* Aspirin comes in small tins of twenty-five, in bottles of fifty, one hundred, and one hundred fifty. Whew!

That's a lot of headaches! And they're all very tightly wrapped. I wonder if I should get the kind that comes in capsules instead of the tablet type. This is handy! They've got the price-per-hundred posted under each size and brand for comparison. I think I'll try this "house" brand. As long as they're all five grains or three hundred twenty-five milligrams, one aspirin is probably just as good as another.

PHARMACIST: Mr. Binns, I've got the drug your doctor ordered in stock. Your prescription will be ready in about ten minutes. My new assistant, Bill Delaney, will take care of it as soon as he finishes a few others he's working on. In the meantime, is there anything else I can help you with?

MR. BINNS: Yes, I believe there is. My wife has added vitamin C to the list we made. I believe in taking vitamins to supplement one's diet, but I'd like your opinion.

PHARMACIST: Vitamin C is certainly one of the most important of the basic vitamin groups which our bodies need, but it's not the only one. If you two are serious about taking vitamins to supplement your regular diet, I suggest you try one of these multivitamins.

MR. BINNS: What are the advantages?

PHARMACIST: Depending on which brand—and on how much you want to spend—you can get a dozen or more minerals and vitamins which the body needs. I recommend that you discuss this with your doctor before you decide.

MR. BINNS: That sounds like good advice. I also want to ask you about these new diet pills. I've seen them advertised on TV and in magazines.

PHARMACIST: Well, again, I suggest checking with your doctor.

These appetite suppressant pills can have some dangerous side effects on some people. I'd rather not sell them to you until you check it out with someone who knows your medical history.

MR. BINNS: Thanks, Mr. Kreck. As always, you're more interested in the well-being of your customers than in just making a sale. But I'm not going to let you talk me out of buying a new toothbrush. My old one is worn out, and I need a new one. What do you recommend?

PHARMACIST: Here's a good one. It's sturdy, yet the bristles are soft, which is good for stimulating your gums as well as brushing your teeth. These are on sale this week. You even get your choice of colors.

MR. BINNS: Thanks. I'll take the red one, and I'd better pick up some toothpaste while I'm here.

ASSISTANT: Mr. Binns, your prescription is ready.

PHARMACIST: Mr. Binns, I'd like you to meet my new helper, Bill Delaney. Bill, this is Mr. Binns, an old and valued customer.

MR. BINNS: Oh, I'm not as old as I look. Pleased to meet you, Bill.

ASSISTANT: It's good to meet you, Mr. Binns. By the way, did you know that we were having a special on film-developing this week? If you have any film you want processed, this is the time to do it.

MR. BINNS: I wonder why they call this a *drug*store?

COMPREHENSION AND CONVERSATION PRACTICE

1. Where does this dialogue take place? What people take part in the dialogue?
2. What items did Mr. Binns have on his shopping list?
3. What did he discover about the packaging of aspirin?
4. What is a *house* brand?
5. What's the difference between a *capsule* and a *tablet?*
6. Do you ever take aspirin? What brand do you use?
7. What is a *pharmacist?* What are a pharmacist's duties?
8. Have you ever had a prescription filled? Where?
9. Are prescription medicines expensive? Why?
10. Why are some drugs sold only by prescription?
11. What are *over-the-counter* medicines?
12. What happens when film is processed or developed?
13. Give an example of a side effect a medicine might have on someone.
14. What are diet pills supposed to do?
15. Explain what Mr. Binns meant by his last remark.

VOCABULARY PRACTICE

1. Which of these words forms its plural with an *s* and which form their plurals by changing the *f* to *v* and adding *es?* (shelf, half, chief, wife)
2. A *multivitamin* has (only vitamin C, many vitamins, no vitamins, an appetite suppressant).
3. When you *fill a prescription,* you (pour water into it, take a pill with water, have a pharmacist prepare it, write to the doctor).
4. *Diet* rhymes with (quiet, height, riot, Viet, spite, rein).
5. If something costs six dollars for one hundred fifty, what is the price per hundred? ($2, $3, $4, $5)
6. An *assistant* is (an aide, a hindrance, a competitor, a pharmacist).
7. Ten minutes *or so* means (ten minutes exactly, less than ten minutes, more than ten minutes, about ten minutes).
8. A *house brand* is (furniture, an expensive car, a small plant, a

commercial product that is less expensive because it is not advertised).
9. An undesirable secondary reaction is (an also-ran, a side effect, a second chance, a bad habit).
10. A complete summary of a person's illnesses is called (a laundry list, a medical history, a clinical run-down, hospital corners).

Use Each of These Phrases in a Sentence

if you will • wait just a minute • to pick up • I wonder • to come in • Whew! • to be handy • as long as • to take care of • in the meantime • as to • check it out • a good buy

The Sheraton Corporation

unit (15)

Staying at a Motel

LOUIS: I think we'd better stop for the night soon, dear. I'm getting tired of driving. You look as though you're done in too.

CARMEN: I am. Ten hours on the road is long enough for anyone, especially in this heat. I'm anxious to get to Mom's, but I don't think we should overdo it. We should be rested when we arrive, or we won't have a good visit.

LOUIS: I agree. Why don't you look in the travel guide to see if it recommends any motels along this road. The last sign we passed said that there were a few small towns up ahead. There will probably be some motels. Well, look at that! No sooner do we start to look for a motel, when one appears. Let's pull over and have a look.

CARMEN: Uh-oh, a "No Vacancy" sign. I hope we don't run

into that problem. I'd hate to sleep in the car all night.

LOUIS: I'm sure we won't have to. What does the book say?

CARMEN: There are three listed. That one we just passed was one of them. Let's look at the other two and hope they aren't filled as well. The second has a cute-sounding name and the third is part of a large chain. Turn right at that road up there. The cute one should be about half a mile down that road. It's not far.

LOUIS: Well, what do you think? It looks a bit run-down to me, but at least their "Vacancy" sign is on.

CARMEN: No, I don't like this one. If the larger one is filled, we can come back here, but it's a little too seedy for my taste. Let's go on. The chain has such a good reputation that I'd feel a lot better there.

LOUIS: There it is. We're in luck; let's check in. *(They drive up to the door marked "office," park the car, and go in to register.)* Good afternoon.

CLERK: Good evening, sir, ma'am. Just the two of you?

LOUIS: Yes. We'd like a single for one night. Do you have one available?

CLERK: Just one, and it only became available a few minutes ago. A couple on their way to Salt Lake City had a reservation, but they called to say they couldn't make it. This is a busy time of the year. You're lucky you found this one. Please fill out this registration card and be sure to list your car's license number. Will you be paying by credit card?

LOUIS: Yes. Here. *(The desk clerk runs the card through the machine and hands a paper across the desk for a signature.)*

CLERK: You're in room 27. It's around the back, past the swimming pool. You can back your car right up to the door. The restaurant closes at 9:30, but the bar stays open until midnight. The snack bar opens for breakfast at 6:00 a.m. Enjoy your stay. *(He hands them a key and they leave.)*

LOUIS: Pleasant fellow.

CARMEN: Yes. A little brusque, but I suppose he has to give all that information dozens of times a day. I'm looking forward to a bath and relaxing in an air-conditioned room.

LOUIS: I think I'll change into my bathing suit right away and go for a refreshing swim. Ah, this is the best part of the day. Let's be sure to get to the dining room before it closes. I'm really hungry already; by the time I have a swim, I'll probably be starving.

CARMEN: Look, there's a sign on the door of room 27. It says "Welcome, weary travelers." That's us!

COMPREHENSION AND CONVERSATION PRACTICE

1. Where does this dialogue take place? What people take part in the dialogue?
2. How long had the couple been traveling? Where were they going?
3. What does *No Vacancy* mean?
4. As the words relate to motel rooms, what do *single* and *double* mean?
5. Have you ever stayed in a motel? When? Where?
6. How are motels different from hotels?
7. What are the names of some motel chains that you know?

8. Which credit cards do most motels accept for payment?
9. What time of the year do you think it is in the dialogue?
10. What time of year is the busiest for motels?
11. What information do registration cards ask for?
12. Besides a pool and a restaurant, what other facilities do most motels offer?
13. What makes one place look acceptable and another look seedy?
14. What type of personality would a person need to work in a motel?
15. How did the word *motel* come into the language?

VOCABULARY PRACTICE

1. Along with *dear*, which of these terms are also words of endearment which people in love often call each other? (darling, sweetheart, clerk, dummy, honey)
2. To *be in luck* is to (have good fortune, be in a motel, be ill, be tired).
3. Which of these words does *not* rhyme with all the others? (passed, past, last, mast, based)
4. *Seedy* means (having growth potential, quiet, dirty, silly, funny).
5. *Brusque* means (pleasant, heavy, blunt, well-groomed).
6. *No sooner* means (before, at the same time, two days after, just after).
7. To *have a look* means to (stare, check, put on your glasses).
8. A *bathing suit* is used for (bathing, riding, skiing, swimming).
9. A person who *overdoes it* will probably be (rested, refreshed, weary, relaxed).
10. To *run into* a problem is to (drive over it, trip over it, have to confront it, avoid it).

Use Each of These Phrases in a Sentence
for the night • to get tired • to be done in • no sooner . . . than • to have a look • cute-sounding • run-down • at least • in luck • to check in • couldn't make it

unit (16)

Hickey-Freeman Company

Buying a Suit

CUSTOMER: I saw your ad in this morning's paper. It looks like you've got some good buys on men's suits.

CLERK: Yes, sir. Right this way, please. Let's see. You look like a 40 Regular. Is that right?

CUSTOMER: Usually I'm a 38 Regular, but it's true that I've gained a little weight lately. How can you tell a person's size that way?

CLERK: After you've been in the business as long as I have, it's not difficult, believe me. Here, try this coat on just for size. We'll see if you have indeed grown into a new size. We'll try a 38 first.

CUSTOMER: It's pretty snug. I guess you're right. I'll try a 40.

CLERK: That looks as though it were made for you. How does it feel?

CUSTOMER: Perfect. So, a 40 it is. What I'd like to look at is a dark, business-type suit—the kind that never goes out of style. Something in wool, I think.

CLERK: Right this way. We have some excellent pure wool suits. Wool has the best of everything—more comfort, more quality, more value. But as to style, I think you should realize that even the most conservative styles still change. The width of lapels changes, the number of buttons in front and on sleeves changes, even the number of pockets changes.

CUSTOMER: I'm sure you're right. It's just that I dread the idea of buying a new suit every year.

CLERK: Well, the changes are not usually that dramatic. What do you think of this one with a faint pinstripe?

CUSTOMER: No, that's a bit too formal for me. I'd like something dark but not stodgy: a dark grey, or navy blue, or even black. But I prefer a solid color.

CLERK: Black might be too solemn for someone your age. Here, try this three-piece grey worsted. Worsteds are nice and warm. You can use the dressing room over there to try it on, if you'd like. *(A few minutes later, the customer is standing in front of a mirror outside the dressing room. He is admiring the cut of the suit.)* That looks almost tailor-made for you. We can take these sleeves up a bit, hem the trousers of course, and perhaps take in a tuck at the waist. What do you think?

CUSTOMER: It's just what I wanted. I can't believe that buying a suit can be this easy. The last time I bought a suit, it took me hours to decide, and I visited several different stores. How long will it take for the alterations?

CLERK: *(He uses a soft piece of chalk to mark where the alterations are to be made.)* We have a seamstress here in the store. We don't have to send any work out. Your suit should be ready in a day or so. I'll call you when it's ready.

CUSTOMER: That's great. I'll need some new clothes for a party this weekend.

CLERK: It will definitely be ready by the weekend, I can promise that.

CUSTOMER: Can I charge this?

CLERK: Yes, but before you do, let's look at some accessories. I've got a fine selection of ties to go with that new suit, and in other sections of the store, we've got shirts, belts, socks, sweaters, . . .

CUSTOMER: Wait a minute! I'd better check my budget. I do need some of those items you've mentioned, but I'm not sure I can afford them at this time.

COMPREHENSION AND CONVERSATION PRACTICE

1. Where does this dialogue take place? What people take part in the dialogue?
2. What are some materials used in men's suits?
3. Is wool usually a light or heavy material? How does it differ from polyester materials?
4. What are the three pieces of a three-piece suit?
5. What size suit do you wear? Your father? Your brother?
6. What are some examples of alterations often made on a suit?
7. Describe the latest fashion in men's suits.
8. What is a *pinstripe?*
9. What else does a men's store sell besides suits?
10. Name some stores which sell men's clothing near your home.

11. How much would you expect to pay for a good men's wool suit?
12. Do men's clothes cost more than women's? Why/Why not?
13. What are the most popular colors of men's clothes in your country?
14. What is your favorite color for a man's suit? What is your favorite style?
15. What does *tailor-made* mean?

VOCABULARY PRACTICE

1. Which of the following are somber colors? (brown, pink, black, grey)
2. The opposite of *snug* is (tight, new, loose, asleep).
3. A suit made from firm-textured yarn is a (dark, dramatic, worsted, colorful) suit.
4. A common synonym for *trousers* is (vest, pants, sleeves, lapel).
5. What is the noun form of these verbs? (alter, hem, admire, decide, mark)
6. The *style* of a suit can also be called its (length, width, hem, cut).
7. A *belt* goes around a (sleeve, waist, lapel, pocket).
8. To *take in* means to (reduce in size, lengthen, enlarge, add pockets).
9. The word *dread* rhymes with (creed, trade, spread, deed).
10. When you *send work out,* you (throw it away, mail it, do it yourself, hire someone else to do work for you).

Use Each of These Phrases in a Sentence
tailor-made • right this way • How can you tell? • believe me • formal • try it on • to send work out • it took me • wait a minute • I'm not sure

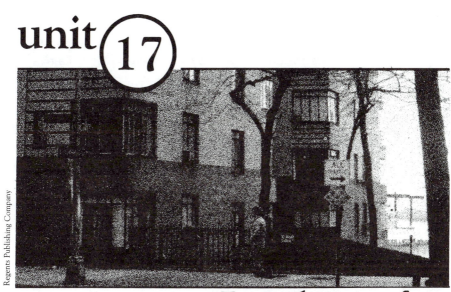

Regents Publishing Company

Looking for an Apartment

MS. BLACK: I'm here to see the apartment that you advertised. I'm Cheryl Black; I called you earlier. You must be Mr. . . . ?

MR. HUDSON: Hudson. Jerome Hudson. I'm the resident manager. Let me get the key. The apartment is on the fourth floor. The previous tenant just moved out yesterday, so we haven't cleaned it or repainted it yet. Please ignore the mess; we'll have it ready for occupancy within the week.

MS. BLACK: My roommate and I have a lease in our present place until the end of the month, so we wouldn't be ready to move for a few weeks; that is, if we decide we like this one. Have many people come to see it?

MR. HUDSON: No, you're the first. *(They ride the elevator up to the fourth floor.)* It's right down this hall. The laundry room and the trash room are both in the basement. The elevator is self-service, so it operates twenty-four hours a day, and there's also a stairway at the other end of the hall.

MS. BLACK: How is the mail delivered?

MR. HUDSON: There are boxes in the lobby. I'll show you when we go back downstairs. Here we are. Apartment 407. *(They enter.)* This is the living room-dining room combination. All the apartments in this building have this L-shaped arrangement. If you open the windows at either end of the living room area, there's a good cross breeze on most days. It's good ventilation.

MS. BLACK: Where's the kitchen?

MR. HUDSON: Right around here. It's small, but fully equipped. The dishwasher is new, and the stove is less than a year old. The refrigerator is self-defrosting. The switch for the garbage disposal is here over the sink.

MS. BLACK: Is there air conditioning? I know you said the ventilation is good, but I know how hot it can get in the city during the summer.

MR. HUDSON: Yes, there's central air conditioning and central heating. The thermostat which controls both is here in the hallway. You don't have any pets, do you? We don't allow pets.

MS. BLACK: No, neither of us has a pet. Does the rent include utilities?

MR. HUDSON: It includes water and gas but not electricity, and, of course, it doesn't include your telephone. The walls are not entirely soundproof, so we ask that you not play your stereo, radio, or TV too loud after 10:00 p.m.

MS. BLACK: I'd like to look at the bedrooms and the bathroom, please.

MR. HUDSON: This is the larger bedroom. It has a walk-in closet and its own half bath. It's a little more private than the other bedroom.

MS. BLACK: Oh, I can see Cindy and me fighting over who gets which room already.

MR. HUDSON: The former tenant, a single man, used the second bedroom as an office. He was a free-lance writer, and he used the room to work in.

MS. BLACK: Why did he move?

MR. HUDSON: He couldn't pay the rent, so we had to ask him to leave.

MS. BLACK: Speaking of the rent, when is it due? And how much security deposit do you require?

MR. HUDSON: The rent is due no later than the fifth of the month, but we prefer to have it on the first. We ask that you leave a month's rent as a security deposit. It will be returned to you at the end of your lease.

MS. BLACK: Is there any storage area?

MR. HUDSON: There are bins for each apartment in the basement next to the laundry room. We recommend that you buy a lock for your bin, and that you not keep any-thing valuable in it.

MS. BLACK: I like the apartment, Mr. Hudson. I'll talk it over with Cindy and bring her by to see it for herself. I'm sure she'll like it too. I'll call you to arrange a time for her to see it.

COMPREHENSION AND CONVERSATION PRACTICE

1. Where does this dialogue take place? What people take part in the dialogue?
2. What is a *resident manager?*
3. How does this apartment differ from yours (or from one you know about)?
4. What is *cross ventilation?* Why is it important?
5. What appliances are you likely to find in a *fully-equipped* kitchen?
6. What is a *laundry room?* What machines are in one?
7. What types of pets do people have in apartments?
8. What kind of pet do you have? What kind would you like to have?
9. What are *utilities?*
10. How much does electricity cost? How is it measured?
11. What is a security deposit used for?
12. What is a *free-lance* writer?
13. How long is a normal lease for? What happens when a lease expires?
14. What are some items you might keep in an apartment storage area?
15. Make a drawing of how you think the apartment in the dialogue looks.

VOCABULARY PRACTICE

1. To *ignore* is to (overlook, look over, pay attention to, talk to).
2. Meals are usually eaten in the (bedroom, dining room, living room, kitchen).
3. The opposite of *valuable* is (worthy, worthless, valued, valiant).
4. A *lease* is (a room, an apartment, a tenant, a rental agreement).
5. You would probably put your dirty dishes in the (disposal, stove, dishwasher, refrigerator).
6. If something is *private,* it is (physically comfortable, ugly, luxurious, secluded).

7. *Quote* rhymes with (route, vote, bout, root).
8. To *allow* is to (disagree, permit, wonder, go up).
9. To *talk* something *over* is to (reject it, doubt it, insist on it, discuss it).
10. Give the meanings of these two-word verbs: bring by, bring up, bring over, bring out, bring on.

Use Each of These Phrases in a Sentence

to move out • to have something ready • self-service • L-shaped • central heating • not entirely • to look at • walk-in • to fight over • to work in • speaking of • no later than

Wendy's International

Eating at a Fast-food Restaurant

MYRTLE: Have you eaten here before?

LILLIAN: No. I've tried several fast-food places in the neigh-
           borhood, but I haven't ever been here. In fact, I
           don't recognize this one. Is it new?

MYRTLE: Yes. It's a new chain. They specialize in ham-
           burgers and chicken. I guess it's not much different
           from all the others, except, of course, for the ones
           that only do fish dishes. Anyway, I thought we'd try
           it. They're having an introductory special. You get
           free french fries with every sandwich order. I have
           this coupon.

LILLIAN: Do you have an extra one for me?

MYRTLE: No, only this one.

LILLIAN: Maybe I'll try their hot pie instead of having french
           fries. This is a long line, but it seems to be moving

fast. Do you know what you're going to order yet?

MYRTLE: Not yet. I'm interested in the chicken platter, though. The sign says you get two pieces of fried chicken, a soft drink, a hot roll, and a trip to the salad bar. All that along with my potatoes! Sounds mouth-watering, doesn't it?

LILLIAN: Not to me. I don't care for fried chicken. I think I'll try their bacon cheeseburger.

CLERK: Hello there, folks! What can I get for you today?

LILLIAN: I'll have the bacon cheeseburger, a side order of cole slaw, and a vanilla milk shake, please.

CLERK: As an unadvertised special, you can have a trip to the salad bar with your order for only a dollar more.

LILLIAN: No, thanks, this will be enough.

MYRTLE: I'm going to have the chicken platter with a small cola, and please don't put any ice in my soft drink. Oh, and here's my coupon for a free small order of fries. Here, take both of our orders out of this. Do we get discounts for being senior citizens? *(She hands the clerk a ten-dollar bill.)*

CLERK: Yes, you do. All our stores offer a ten-percent discount on all purchases over five dollars for people over sixty-five, but I must say that neither of you looks old enough to be called "senior."

LILLIAN: You're too kind. Thank you, young lady.

CLERK: Will this be to go or will you be eating here?

MYRTLE: We'll eat here.

CLERK: While you're waiting for your order, here are two of

our big prize game cards. You have to scratch the surface of the card and match the number which appears with one of the prize-winning numbers up there on our bulletin board. You could win up to ten thousand dollars.

MYRTLE: Oh, I never win anything.

CLERK: *(She prepares their order.)* Who knows? You might get lucky this time. I'd like to draw your attention to our breakfast menu up there over the food counter. If you're ever in the mood for a fast and easy breakfast out, we have a wide selection which we serve from 6:30 to 10:30 a.m. Here you are. Your order is ready. Enjoy your meal and have a nice day.

COMPREHENSION AND CONVERSATION PRACTICE

1. Where does this dialogue take place? What people take part in the dialogue?
2. What is *fast food?*
3. What are the names of some fast-food chains in your area?
4. Have you ever eaten at a fast-food place? Which? Which is your favorite?
5. What are *french fries?* What other ways are there to prepare potatoes?
6. What is your favorite way to cook potatoes?
7. What are some examples of fast-food fish dishes?
8. What are *coupons?* How are they used?
9. What are some ways (in addition to frying) of preparing chicken?
10. Describe a bacon cheeseburger.
11. What condiments do people usually put on their burgers?
12. What types of items might you find at a salad bar?
13. What is a *senior citizen?*
14. Do you ever win anything in games such as the one described in the dialogue?
15. What items would you expect to find on a fast-food restaurant's breakfast menu?

VOCABULARY PRACTICE

1. The abbreviation *a.m.* means (morning, afternoon, evening, night).
2. Ten percent of five dollars is (5¢, 50¢, $1, $50).
3. All of the following, except one, is a fish dish: shrimp, clams, chicken, cod, haddock.
4. *Mouth-watering* means (wet, dry, hot, delicious).
5. To *scratch* the surface of something is to (eat, scrape, prepare, order) it.
6. A company with many outlets to sell things such as food is called a (chain, salad bar, fast-food place, senior citizen).
7. The meal that people eat in the morning is called (lunch, dinner, breakfast, snacks).
8. A list of available food dishes is called a (bill, menu, board, card).
9. *Cole slaw* is made from (cabbage, potatoes, hamburger, salad).
10. You're *too* kind means you're (not, sometimes, never, very) kind.

Use Each of These Phrases in a Sentence

to specialize in • different from • anyway • an extra one • not yet • along with • to go (food) • Who knows? • to draw one's attention to • have a nice day

unit (19)

The Sheraton Corporation

Dining at an Expensive Restaurant

BLANCHE: Are you sure we can afford to eat here? It looks so expensive.

WILLIAM: Don't worry about it. It's our anniversary, and we should celebrate.

BLANCHE: You're right. We deserve a splendid meal on such an occasion. I look forward to this evening. I've heard excellent things about the food here.

HOSTESS: Good evening. Do you have a reservation?

WILLIAM: Yes, we do. It's for two people, in the name of Dubois.

HOSTESS: Come with me, please. *(She leads them to a candlelit table for two in a far corner of the dining room.)* Your waiter will be with you in a moment. Would you care for a cocktail?

WILLIAM: Yes, I believe I'll have a piña colada. I understand it's your specialty.

BLANCHE: I'll have a whiskey sour. We're celebrating our anniversary.

HOSTESS: I'll make sure the bartender makes his finest drinks to help your celebration.

BLANCHE: I feel so pampered already. This is really an elegant place.

WAITER: Good evening. My name is René. I'll be serving you this evening. May I bring you the menu now?

WILLIAM: Yes, please. *(The waiter brings the menu and a wine list.)*

WILLIAM: I don't think we'll want any wine with dinner. These cocktails are quite enough. We'll look over the menu for a few minutes.

WAITER: Very good, sir. The lobster and the prime rib are both excellent this evening, if I may recommend them.

WILLIAM: Thank you, René. *(The waiter leaves.)* I'm not going to look at the right side of the menu. I'm just going to order whatever looks good.

BLANCHE: Good idea. Me too. I think I'll start with an appetizer of oysters Rockefeller. I've always wanted to try that dish.

WILLIAM: That sounds good, but I think I'll have the French onion soup. I'm also going to have an artichoke salad, but I can't decide what I want for my main course. The duck in orange sauce looks tempting.

BLANCHE: I'm leaning toward the New York cut steak. It says

it comes with a baked potato and a choice of vegetable. I think I'll try their three-lettuce salad with house dressing. Fran told me she tried it last week when she was here with her fiancé. Everything looks so good. I'm also tempted to take our waiter's advice and try the prime rib.

WAITER: Have you decided or would you like some more time?

BLANCHE: We know what we want for our appetizers and for our salads, but all of the entrees look so good that we can't decide what to choose.

WAITER: The chef tells me that the veal is particularly tender this evening. He makes a superb veal in butter sauce which he calls Le Papillon. I, myself, have some whenever he finds sufficiently tender meat.

BLANCHE: René, you sound so enthusiastic, I'm going to try it. You've talked me into it. *(They order their meals.)*

WAITER: Was everything satisfactory, madam? Sir?

BLANCHE: Everything was wonderful. It couldn't have been better.

WAITER: We have a complete selection of pastries, if you'd care for some dessert.

WILLIAM: Just some coffee for me, thank you.

BLANCHE: I don't want anything sweet, but I do want something to round out the meal. What do you suggest, René?

WAITER: Perhaps a tray with a small selection of cheeses and fruit would please you.

BLANCHE: Perhaps it would. I'll try that, and I'll have coffee too. Make that cappuccino, instead.

WILLIAM: This has been a splendid evening: great atmosphere, excellent food, and a wonderful dinner partner.

BLANCHE: Happy anniversary.

COMPREHENSION AND CONVERSATION PRACTICE

1. Where does this dialogue take place? What people take part in the dialogue?
2. Have you ever eaten in an expensive restaurant? Where?
3. Why do people need reservations for good restaurants?
4. What is the function of a hostess in a restaurant?
5. When you eat in a restaurant, what is your favorite appetizer? Soup? Salad?
6. Which of the entrees mentioned sounded the most interesting to you?
7. What are some typical entrees found in restaurants in your area?
8. What desserts are usually served in a typical North American restaurant?
9. What is your favorite dessert?
10. How much should one tip a waiter or waitress in a good restaurant?
11. How much would you have tipped René?
12. How much would you expect to pay for a meal such as the one described in the dialogue?
13. Name some cocktails such as those in the dialogue.
14. What kind of meat is *veal? Prime rib? New York cut steak?*
15. Name all of the various courses which are served in an elegant meal.

VOCABULARY PRACTICE

1. An *anniversary* celebration often commemorates a (birthday, wedding, death, graduation).
2. A person who mixes alcoholic drinks is called a (waiter, hostess, bartender, chef).
3. Which of the following is considered seafood? (veal, lobster, steak, duck)
4. *Cappuccino* is a way of preparing (salad, cheese, fruit, coffee).
5. A *fiancé* is someone you are engaged (to, with, by, for).
6. The right side of the menu lists the (salads, prices, dates, wines).
7. To be *pampered* is to be (spoiled, old, young, tempted).
8. *Oysters* are a kind of (vegetable, meat, seafood, dessert).
9. If you *lean toward* something, you are about to (reject it, choose it, enjoy it, leave it).
10. *Pastries* are usually (sour, salty, spicy, sweet).

Use Each of These Phrases in a Sentence

don't worry about it • to look forward to • in the name of • would you care for • to make sure • me too • to lean toward • you talked me into it • it couldn't have been better • to round out • happy anniversary

Regents Publishing Company

unit ⃝20

Reading Ads in the Newspaper

LARRY: Do you have the sports section, Ed?

ED: I didn't know you were interested in sports, Larry.

LARRY: Actually, I'm not. It's just that I need some new snow tires before the winter season is on us full force. I put it off at the end of last winter, and now my tires are practically bald.

ED: How will the sports section of the daily newspaper help that problem?

LARRY: Haven't you ever noticed? The ads that have anything to do with cars are always on the second and third pages of the sports section. Tune-ups, batteries, tires, mufflers—you name it—the sales and special offers are all there.

ED: Come to think of it, you're right. I'll bet there are a lot of other ads that always appear in the same section of the newspaper too.

LARRY: Sure. Restaurants always try to entice us in the entertainment section, right near the movie and theater ads. I suppose it's a natural link; if you go out to a film, you might want to eat first. Of course, the movies themselves are advertised in that section too. The big-budget films sometimes take out full-page ads telling us why we should go to see them.

ED: I've noticed that TV shows are advertising these days too.

LARRY: The ratings are so important that they'll try all sorts of approaches to build their audience.

ED: I've noticed that you've started to clip coupons from the food section of the paper. I've often thought that it would be a good idea to do that, but I guess I've been too lazy. Do you think it pays off?

LARRY: If you mean—do I think it's a good idea to cut out money-saving coupons?—the answer is "yes." I figure that we're going to buy the food anyway, so why not find a more economical way to do it? It's not really too much trouble. I scan the ads to see if anything is on sale that we need. Since we have a freezer, it's a good idea to buy some items when they're on sale and freeze them for later use. The whole operation of scanning, clipping, and keeping the "cents-off" coupons in a special drawer doesn't take more than a few minutes a week.

ED: Well, my hat's off to you for being so thrifty and conscientious. Speaking of saving money, did you see that the appliance store was having a sale on video cassette recorders? I've always wanted one, and now maybe I can afford one.

LARRY: No, I didn't, but I did see something interesting in the classified ads today. I was looking under "Mer-

chandise" for a used typewriter. I didn't see anything that interested me, but at the end of that
column I saw that there was going to be a com-
munity rummage sale at the civic center on Saturday.

ED: I like going to yard sales. One person's trash is
another person's treasures, I've always said.

LARRY: This is supposed to be the largest yard sale of the
year. I'm going to get there early so I can get the
pick of the junk.

ED: While we're on the subject of sales, have you seen
any advertisements for contact lenses? Someone
told me there was a new optician in the neighborhood who was offering a good deal on contacts. I
need an extra pair, and I don't want to pay full price
if I don't have to.

LARRY: No, I haven't, but I think your best bet would be to
look carefully in the front section, where all the
national and international news is. For some rea-
son, ads for clothes, shoes, and eyeglasses seem
to be in that part. On the other hand, if you wait
until Sunday, I'm sure you won't have any trouble
finding some reference to what you're looking for.
There are advertising supplements in the larger
Sunday paper.

ED: The next time I want to buy something, I'm going
to look thoroughly in the newspaper to see if someone, somewhere is advertising it. Now, do you
know where the business section is? I want to
check today's ads for the price of gold.

COMPREHENSION AND CONVERSATION PRACTICE

1. Where does this dialogue take place? What people take part in the dialogue?
2. What is the name of your daily newspaper? Are there many ads in it?
3. What ads appear in the sports section regularly?
4. What ads appear regularly in the entertainment section?
5. Where are you likely to find department store sale advertisements?
6. Do restaurants advertise regularly in newspapers?
7. Do movie or TV ads influence you?
8. What is the value of advertising?
9. Can advertising ever be harmful?
10. What are *cents-off* coupons? How are they used?
11. What are *classified* ads? Besides used merchandise, what are some examples of classified ads?
12. Where do *help-wanted* ads appear in the newspaper?
13. What's the difference between an optician and an optometrist?
14. Describe the Sunday newspaper in your area. How is it different from the daily paper?
15. What is your favorite section of the newspaper?

VOCABULARY PRACTICE

1. To *entice* means to (lure, ask, advertise, check).
2. "A confusion of miscellaneous articles" defines (merchandise, tires, rummage, freezers).
3. The opposite of *thrifty* is (sparing, wasteful, forty, solid).
4. A common synonym for *trash* is (treasures, merchandise, articles, junk).
5. To *put* something *off* is to (welcome it, postpone it, want it, reject it).
6. If something *pays off,* it (is valueless, has money, needs clipping, is worth it).
7. To inspect something superficially and quickly is to (see it, look at it, scan it, sell it).

8. A tire that is *practically bald* has (a lot of rubber, little tread, no advertising, no hair).
9. *Contact lenses* are worn in one's (cameras, eyes, shoes, clothes).
10. If you got a *good deal* on a purchase, you would be (sad, perplexed, satisfied, troubled).

Use Each of These Phrases in a Sentence

it's just that • full force • you name it • come to think of it • to take out (ads) • all sorts of • to pay off • my hat's off to you • best bet • on the other hand

Metropolitan Transportation Authority

Riding the Bus

DRIVER: Stand back from the door, please. Let the passengers off. You can't get on until the other passengers get off.

RIDER #1: How much is the fare, please?

DRIVER: One dollar. Drop it in the box. Move to the rear of the bus. There are plenty of seats in the rear.

RIDER #1: Wait. I want to ask you if this bus goes down Fifth Avenue as far as Greenwich Village.

DRIVER: That's right. Move along, please. There are more people waiting to get on. Move to the rear.

RIDER #1: I thought this bus went down Park Avenue.

DRIVER: No, that's the Number 1. That goes down Park. This is a Number 2.

RIDER #1:   But I thought this was the right bus to go to Washington Square Park.

DRIVER: It is . Get in, please. You're holding everyone up. You can't miss Washington Square Park.

RIDER #1:   Would you tell me when we get there?

DRIVER: It would be better if you watched out for yourself. I might forget.

RIDER #1:   Well, how will I recognize it?

DRIVER: Just watch for the big arch and all the trees. Get off the bus when we get there. Come on. Keep moving. I haven't got all day.

RIDER #1:   You don't have to be so rude. I only asked you a simple question.

DRIVER: And I only gave you a simple answer. I don't have time to have a long conversation with every person that gets on the bus. Can't you see the line of people behind you? You're attracting a bigger crowd than the mayor.

RIDER #2:   I know what the fare is for me, but what about my two sons? How much do I have to pay for them?

DRIVER: Full fare for the older one. The little guy rides free as long as he doesn't take the seat of a full-fare passenger.

RIDER #2:   Would you point out the Metropolitan Museum as we go by?

DRIVER: Look, this isn't a sight-seeing bus. It's at Eighty-fourth Street. Sit on the right side of the bus, if there's a seat. You'll see it as we go by. It's a big building. You can't miss it.

RIDER #2:   On the right side?

DRIVER: That's right.

RIDER #2:   Also, we'd like some transfers for the Thirty-fourth Street crosstown bus. How much extra is that?

DRIVER: There's no charge for transfers. Here. Step along. Have your fares ready as you get on the bus. Would somebody give this young boy a hand? He's limping and having a hard time getting on. You're the last passenger, son. That's it! I'm closing the doors. Move back. Another bus will be along in a few minutes.

RIDER #3:   Thank you. I've got a cast on my foot. It's hard to get around sometimes. You're very kind. *(He drops his fare into the box.)*

DRIVER: Okay, let's clear a seat for this kid. Those seats are for the elderly and the handicapped. You'll have to move over. Okay, son, just squeeze through. They're making room for you now. *(Before pulling away from the curb, he opens the door again.)* Okay, push in a little bit, everybody. Let the lady in. There's always room for one more.

COMPREHENSION AND CONVERSATION PRACTICE

1. Where does this dialogue take place? What people take part in the dialogue?
2. According to the dialogue, what is the fare on the Fifth Avenue bus?
3. What other means of transportation do you know of in New York City?
4. What is the fare for public transportation in your town?
5. Do you ride a bus regularly? Where do you get on and off?
6. Do the buses in your town stop at every corner or only at specially marked stations?

7. Why does the driver in the dialogue keep asking the people to move to the rear of the bus?
8. Is it easy to be a bus driver?
9. On most buses, are transfers free or is there a charge?
10. How do the passengers in the dialogue pay their fare? How do you pay your fare on your city's buses?
11. What is a *sight-seeing* bus?
12. What is the age cut-off for paying full fare or riding free?
13. What is a *handicapped* person?
14. Is the driver in the dialogue typical of most bus drivers you have met?
15. What is your favorite form of public transportation? Why?

VOCABULARY PRACTICE

1. Another word for *riders* is (customers, clients, fans, passengers).
2. The opposite of *rear* is (back, front, side, top).
3. The opposite of *rude* is (polite, loud, raw, long).
4. To *point out* something is to (examine it, enjoy it, miss it, indicate it).
5. How many syllables are in each of these words? (passengers, everyone, village, conversation, metropolitan) Which syllable in each word is stressed?
6. A person boarding a bus gets (up, off, on, to) it.
7. The word *squeeze* rhymes with (lease, please, whiz, his).
8. What you pay when you get on a bus is a (fee, admission, cost, fare).
9. A *mayor* is an elected official who runs a (state, city, county, country).
10. What is the difference in pronunciation between the noun *transfer* and the verb *transfer*?

Use Each of These Phrases in a Sentence
to stand back • how much • in the rear • to hold . . . up • I haven't got all day • can't you see • to go by • no charge • to have a hard time • that's it!

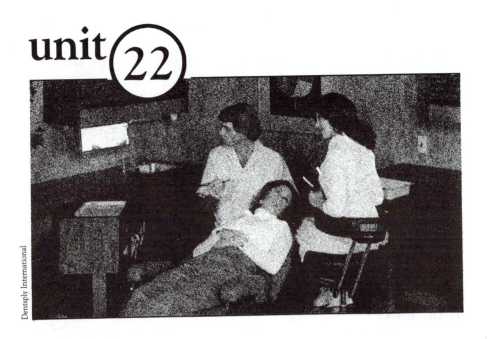

Dentsply International

Visiting the Dentist

MRS. MOORE: Thank you for taking me at the last minute, Doctor.

DR. KANE: It's all right. The last patient left just a moment ago. I don't mind staying late when a regular patient has an emergency.

MRS. MOORE: Where's Miss Perkins? I didn't see her when I came in.

DR. KANE: Not only don't we have a receptionist today, but even my dental assistant has gone home. We're the only ones left, Mrs. Moore. Now, why don't you have a seat and tell me what the problem is.

MRS. MOORE: *(She sits down in the dentist's chair.)* I have a filling which is loose and is about to drop out. I also have a soreness on the side of my mouth. I don't know whether it's from one of my teeth or whether it's a little neuralgia.

DR. KANE: Let me take a look at it. Open your mouth wide, please. On which side of your mouth did you say it hurts you?

MRS. MOORE: Ouch! Ouch! *(She begins to wave her arms violently in great pain.)*

DR. KANE: But, Mrs. Moore, I haven't even touched you yet.

MRS. MOORE: I know, Doctor *(with a sigh of relief)*—but I am so afraid of a dentist that I feel pain even before you touch me.

DR. KANE: I am sorry you feel this way, but let's see what the trouble is.

MRS. MOORE: It's on the left side—just above my eye tooth. The pain seems to skip around—sometimes it is in one place and sometimes in another.

DR. KANE: Does the tooth itself ever ache or become sore to the touch? Is it sensitive to heat or cold?

MRS. MOORE: No, only the gum above the tooth seems to get sore.

DR. KANE: The teeth in that area seem to be sound. It may be a little neuralgia, as you say—but we'd better take an X-ray just to be sure none of the teeth are abscessed. *(He adjusts the machine, takes the picture, etc.)* Now, let's see that loose filling. It's surprising it didn't fall out. There's a good deal of decay around it. There is also a slight cavity on the other side of the tooth which you probably didn't know you had.

MRS. MOORE: Oh, dear, I do hope you won't have to pull the tooth.

DR. KANE: I don't think so. It's not quite as serious as that. But it may take considerable drilling. I'll have to give you an injection of Novocaine. The decay has gone deeply into the tooth. From the size of this hole, I suggest that we cap your tooth, Mrs. Moore. I know it's expensive, but I don't think another filling is going to hold. I can fit you for a permanent cap today and put a temporary one there. Then when the cap is ready, you can come back. Shall I take an impression?

MRS. MOORE: I suppose it's all right. We don't have any dental insurance, but if a cap will save my tooth and stop this pain, then go ahead. Oh, I hate going to the dentist. Uh, nothing personal, Dr. Kane.

DR. KANE: I understand. Many of my patients feel the same way. If I took all expressions of dread personally, I'd never make it as a dentist. Now, open wide. Wider, please. *(He inserts a few wads of cotton into Mrs. Moore's mouth, along with a tube to extract saliva. He probes with a long, sharp pick, and finally, starts drilling.)* Now, let's see what we have here.

COMPREHENSION AND CONVERSATION PRACTICE

1. Where does the dialogue take place? What people take part in the dialogue?
2. Why did Mrs. Moore come so late in the day?
3. Why did she seem to experience great pain even before the dentist opened her mouth?
4. Why did Dr. Kane take an X-ray? What is an X-ray?
5. Have you ever had your mouth X-rayed? Why?
6. When did you last visit the dentist?
7. Do you have many fillings in your teeth?
8. How much do dentists charge for X-rays? For fillings? For caps?
9. What does Novocaine do? How is it usually administered?
10. What other ways do dentists use to alleviate discomfort in their patients?

11. Have you ever had a tooth pulled? Do you have any false teeth?
12. What is the job of a receptionist?
13. What does a dental assistant do?
14. What kinds of materials are used to fill cavities?
15. What is the value of frequent brushing of teeth?

VOCABULARY PRACTICE

1. A dentist refers to those who visit his or her office as (customers, clients, patients, victims).
2. The opposite of *loose* is (tight, open, wide, large).
3. To *dread* something is to (enjoy it, love it, fear it, recognize it).
4. *Considerable* means (some, very little, a great deal, a bit).
5. If something *skips around*, it (begs, seems, stops, moves).
6. The opposite of *extract* is (take out, insert, pull, take).
7. How many teeth are in a perfect set? (20, 24, 28, 32)
8. Give the noun forms of these adjectives: sore, sensitive, sharp, wide.
9. If a tooth is *abscessed*, it is (clean, on the left side, decayed, missing).
10. If you are afraid something is not going to *hold,* you fear that it will (fall out, stay in, grab onto, embrace).

Use Each of These Phrases in a Sentence
last minute • to come in • not only • to take a look at • to have a seat • to skip around • to get sore • to be afraid • to go ahead • to make it • along with

unit (23)

Columbia University/Manny Warman

Watching a Football Game

CARLOS: Thank you for inviting me to the game. In South America, as you know, football is something else entirely.

JEFF: Yes, I know. What you call football, we call soccer. Soccer is gaining in popularity here in the United States, but it's not as popular as football. Practically every high school and college in the country has a team and plays in a league against other teams. And, of course, you know about our professional teams.

CARLOS: Who plays on the professional teams?

JEFF: There are players who have been stars on some university team. After graduation, they become professionals and play football instead of doing some other type of work.

CARLOS: Here comes one of the teams out on the field now. Which team is that?

JEFF: That's the Columbia University team. The players are wearing blue and white jerseys.

CARLOS: Listen to the crowd yell! What enthusiasm there is.

JEFF: The color and the excitement are a very important part of the game. Look at all the young people waving signs and pennants. The Columbia students are all sitting together in the section over there. Those are the cheerleaders down in front. They lead the fans in their school cheers.

CARLOS: It looks like the game is about to start.

JEFF: Yes, there goes the referee's whistle. Both teams are on the field lining up in position for the kickoff. Each team, as you see, has eleven players. There goes the kickoff. The Columbia team is kicking the ball to the opposing team.

CARLOS: I suppose that the idea is for them to catch the ball and carry it to the Columbia goal line. That's similar, of course, to our kind of football, except that we must kick the ball constantly instead of carrying it.

JEFF: The other team has the ball now. The player is running down the field with it. A Columbia player has already tackled him. He didn't get very far with it.

CARLOS: Each of those white lines drawn across the field seems to represent ten yards. Is that right?

JEFF: Yes, the whole field is a hundred yards long. The line across the center of the field is the fifty-yard line and divides the field in half, one half representing the territory of the Columbia team and the other half the territory of the other team.

CARLOS: Both teams are lined up now very close together and facing each other.

JEFF: This is the first play. Each team has a series of special movements, or plays, designed to help them penetrate the line of the other team. Sometimes the plays are very complicated, and the ball is passed from one player to another.

Right now the fullback is plunging through the center of the line. He gained about four yards.

CARLOS: How does the Columbia team finally get possession of the ball?

JEFF: The other team has four tries, or downs, in which to gain ten yards. If they fail to gain, the ball goes over to the opposing team.

CARLOS: One of the players is getting ready to kick the ball. Why is he doing that?

JEFF: The team has been unable to gain their ten yards, and it is now their fourth and last down. Since they are only on their own thirty-yard line, it would be dangerous to give the ball over to Columbia. They will try to kick it deep into Columbia territory. There it goes. That was a good kick—at least fifty yards. There is a Columbia player under it waiting to catch it. There, he has it and he's running down the field! Oh! They tackled him at the thirty-yard line. That was good open field running! Let's see what Columbia will do with the ball.

CARLOS: The players are really tackling each other hard. Do they ever get seriously hurt?

JEFF: Yes, unfortunately, they do. This is a very rough game. Watch! Columbia is trying a pass on first down. It's complete! He's in the clear! He's going all the way! A touchdown on the very first play!

CARLOS: How many points does he score for that?

JEFF: Each touchdown counts six points. After the touchdown, the team which has scored gets a chance to kick the ball between the goal posts for an extra point. Sometimes, when a team is unable to score a touchdown, they can kick the ball from wherever they are. If it goes through the goal posts, it's called a field goal and counts three points.

COMPREHENSION AND CONVERSATION PRACTICE

1. Where does this dialogue take place? What people take part in the dialogue?
2. What is the difference between football and soccer?
3. How many players are there on a football team? On a soccer team?
4. What system of scoring is used in football?
5. What are *cheerleaders?* What is their function?
6. What is a *kickoff?*
7. Describe what it means *to tackle* someone.
8. What does *first down* mean? *Second down?* Etc.
9. How long is a football field?
10. Have you ever played football? Would you like to play on a team?
11. What are some famous university football teams in the United States?
12. What are some famous professional football teams in the United States?
13. How long is a football field? How is it divided?
14. Is football a rough sport? Which sport do you think is the roughest?
15. Are you a sports fan? What sports are your favorite to play? To watch?

VOCABULARY PRACTICE

1. A *pennant* is a (light, brush, banner, sign, advertisement).
2. A school *cheer* is also known as a school (band, yell, slogan, motto).
3. A *bench* is a (reserved seat, pass, sofa, long seat with no back).
4. If you drop the ball, you (fumble, catch, pass, kick) it.
5. People who enthusiastically follow a team are called its (students, players, teams, fans).
6. A touchdown is worth (1, 3, 6, 7) points.
7. What are the opposites of these words? (deep, able, rough, complicated, over, noisy)
8. Each team tried to get the ball over the (goal line, fence, fifty-yard line, goal post) in order to score a touchdown.
9. If a pass is complete, a player has (kicked, caught, scored, tackled) the ball.
10. Form the opposites of these words by adding the necessary prefixes: popular, professional, interesting, complete, similar, complicated, possible, fortunately, able.

Use Each of These Phrases in a Sentence

to play against • to be about to • to line up • to face each other • to get hurt • all the way • to get possession of • to tackle

Harold Naideau

Making a Sales Call

RECEPTIONIST:	Good morning. May I help you?
MR. HEWITT:	I'd like to see Ms. Osteen, please. I spoke with her yesterday by phone, and she said to drop in today sometime between 11:00 and noon.
RECEPTIONIST:	Your name, please?
MR. HEWITT:	Bruce Hewitt. I represent the Mount Hood Office Supply Company.
RECEPTIONIST:	*(She rings Ms. Osteen on the office intercom.)* Ms. Osteen will see you now, Mr. Hewitt. Her office is straight down the hall—the third office on the left. Her name is on the door.
MR. HEWITT:	Thank you. *(Mr. Hewitt walks down the hall, knocks lightly on Ms. Osteen's office door, and opens it.)* Ms. Osteen?

MS. OSTEEN: *(She rises, comes around from behind her desk, and shakes his hand.)* Yes. Mr. Hewitt? Come in, please. Have a seat. *(She indicates a chair and sits across from him.)* I'm afraid I only have a few minutes. An unexpected directors' meeting has been called for 12:00 sharp.

MR. HEWITT: I should have come earlier. As I told you yesterday on the phone, I represent the Mount Hood Office Supply Company. You've already placed several orders with us, and I'm here to try to convince you to place more.

MS. OSTEEN: I like your candor, Mr. Hewitt.

MR. HEWITT: I always come straight to the point. We're a new but growing firm in the area, and we're willing to go out of our way to attract customers away from our competitors. Last week you purchased feeder paper for your word processors and some ledger paper from us. Were you pleased with the products and the service?

MS. OSTEEN: Yes, we were.

MR. HEWITT: Good. We pride ourselves on prompt delivery and only the best products, at the lowest cost to you. I'd like to acquaint you with some of the other products we carry, some that I'm sure you use in considerable quantity. I'll leave this catalog with you, if it's okay. Perhaps you could look it over at your leisure. I'm sure that you can save money and time on anything you buy from us.

MS. OSTEEN: Naturally we're always interested in saving money.

MR. HEWITT: We sell all kinds of stationery supplies: typing paper, staplers, pencil sharpeners, desk sets, file folders—you name it. Our prices are lower than any of our competitors by five to ten percent. Compare the prices in our catalog with the prices you are now paying, and you'll see that I'm right. Also, I'd like to point out that our large warehouse enables us to stock many items that other companies would have to order for you. We have them right there on hand for immediate delivery.

MS. OSTEEN: If what you say is true, I'm sure that we'll be doing a lot of business, Mr. Hewitt. I'll look your catalog over and let you know.

MR. HEWITT: I'd like to leave my card, as well. If you need anything, please don't hesitate to call. Thank you for seeing me. I hope I haven't detained you from your meeting.

SECRETARY: *(The door opens, and Ms. Osteen's secretary walks partway in.)* They're waiting for you at the meeting, Ms. Osteen.

MS. OSTEEN: I'll be right there, Coretta. *(She offers her hand.)* Thanks for dropping in, Mr. Hewitt. It was a pleasure to meet you.

MR. HEWITT: The pleasure was all mine.

COMPREHENSION AND CONVERSATION PRACTICE

1. Where does this dialogue take place? What people take part in the dialogue?
2. Mr. Hewitt never calls himself a salesman, yet we know he is. How?
3. What do you think Ms. Osteen's job with her company is?
4. Why should she place more orders with Mr. Hewitt's company?
5. Why do the two main people in the dialogue use each other's titles and last names instead of first names?
6. Name some of the supplies Mr. Hewitt's firm sells.

7. What other supplies would you expect an office supply company to sell?
8. What is the function of a catalog?
9. Why do business people such as these shake each other's hands?
10. What is the receptionist's job in this story?
11. What does *five to ten percent lower prices* mean?
12. What are *word processors?* How are they valuable for a company?
13. What is *ledger paper* used for?
14. What is a *warehouse?* Why would Mr. Hewitt's company want one?
15. Did you think Mr. Hewitt was a good salesman? What makes a good salesperson?

VOCABULARY PRACTICE

1. The expression *12:00 sharp* means (about 12:00, before 12:00, after 12:00, exactly at 12:00).
2. To *purchase* is to (sell, buy, discount, represent).
3. *In considerable quantity* means (a little, a lot, a few, not many).
4. To *detain* someone is to (entertain, amuse, delay, joke with) him or her.
5. What is the difference between *stationery* and *stationary?*
6. Another phrase meaning *you name it* is (everything, it's your turn, by all means, the pleasure was all mine).
7. If something is *on hand,* it is (easily accessible, missing, straight, old).
8. A person who is forthright, open, and honest could be said to possess (service, promptness, leisure, candor).
9. *Straight* rhymes with all of these words except one: hate, eight, height, wait, bait, crate.
10. Another word for *company* is (Mount Hood, firm, order, competition.

Use Each of These Phrases in a Sentence
to drop in • down the hall • to shake one's hand • to have a seat • straight to the point • to acquaint someone with • you name it • don't hesitate to call • it was a pleasure • the pleasure was all mine

unit 25

American Cancer Society

Visiting a Doctor

DOCTOR: You said on the phone that you were feeling list-less. What's wrong?

ROB: I don't feel good, Doctor. I don't seem to have any energy.

DOCTOR: Can you be more specific?

ROB: It's nothing I can put my finger on specifically. I feel generally run-down, tired all the time; yet I have trouble sleeping.

DOCTOR: Do you eat well? How's your appetite?

ROB: I probably don't eat well. I eat a lot of fried foods and junk food. I don't eat enough fresh vegetables. I don't even eat many cooked vegetables.

DOCTOR: You've gained some weight since I last saw you. According to my chart, you're about twenty pounds overweight. Those junk foods you mentioned aren't helping. Do you exercise?

ROB: Naturally, I'm not as physically active as I used to be. I'm at my office all day long. I have my own business, and I work pretty hard at it.

DOCTOR: I suspect maybe you work too hard at it. Take off your coat and roll up your sleeve, please. I want to check your blood pressure. How old are you, Rob —about fifty?

ROB: I'm fifty-two.

DOCTOR: *(The doctor takes Rob's blood pressure reading.)* Your pressure is high. It's nothing to be alarmed about yet. But I'm going to have to restrict your salt intake and ask you to exercise more. Are you short of breath at all?

ROB: Yes. I sometimes get dizzy after climbing stairs, and I can't walk long distances or lift heavy objects without panting. I probably should give up smoking.

DOCTOR: You're still smoking! After promising to give it up six months ago! Rob, what happened?

ROB: I went to that class that was guaranteed to make a person stop smoking, but then I suffered some business losses and I began to worry. I guess I always associated smoking with worrying, so I started puffing again. The funny thing is now that I've started again, I'm smoking even more than I was before. I'm up to two packs a day now.

DOCTOR: You're worried, you don't sleep well, you smoke two packs of cigarettes a day, you don't exercise, and your diet is terrible. And you wonder why you're not healthy? I wonder why you're not dead!

ROB: Oh, it's not that bad, is it, Doc?

DOCTOR: Almost. We've got to get you back on a healthy track. You were healthy when you were born, you know, Rob. It's unnatural to be unhealthy.

ROB: What can I do?

DOCTOR: You can start by taking your health more seriously than you have been. I'm going to give you a diet plan, and I want you to stick to it. Your heart sounds healthy when I listen to it, but I suspect all that extra weight you're carrying around is putting a strain on it. The diet will help you to lose weight and help to relieve some of the strain. It's a high fiber, low cholesterol, low salt diet. You'll get all the protein and minerals you need with it.

ROB: It's hard to stick to a diet with my busy schedule.

DOCTOR: Your health is more important than your business. The next step will be exercise. I know it's hard to find the time, but you can at least start walking more. If your office is on the third floor, stop taking the elevator up and down; walk the three flights instead. Walk around the block after dinner. Find ways to increase your physical activity every day. Join a swimming club. Swimming a few times a week is the best exercise you can get.

ROB: I joined a health club last year, but I quit because I never had time to go there.

DOCTOR: Find the time. It's important. And for heaven's sake, stop smoking! Back in the old days, we used to call cigarettes "coffin nails" because we knew they weren't good for the health. Now, it's medically proven that they can cause cancer and a host of other things.

ROB: Okay, I'll try again, but I'm not promising. It's a difficult habit to break. What about my run-down feeling? Can you give me something for that problem? There must be some drug I can take.

DOCTOR: I'd rather not give you any drugs, but temporarily, I will give you a prescription for something that will help you sleep. When your diet and exercise program start to improve your health, though, I'm going to take you off the medicine. Do you understand?

ROB: Yes, thanks a lot, Doc. I appreciate what you're saying and doing.

COMPREHENSION AND CONVERSATION PRACTICE

1. Where does this dialogue take place? What people take part in the dialogue?
2. Why was the patient seeing his doctor?
3. What was the doctor's attitude toward the patient's lifestyle and habits?
4. When did you last see a doctor? Why did you go?
5. Do you smoke? What do you think of smoking?
6. What is *blood pressure?* Do you know what your blood pressure reading is?
7. How is salt related to one's blood pressure?
8. Why is high blood pressure bad?
9. What is a *stethoscope?*
10. What other devices does a doctor use to help him or her learn about one's body and its functions?
11. What are some examples of *junk food?*
12. What kinds of exercise do you do?
13. What can a person do to lose weight?
14. Describe a healthy diet.
15. Do you sleep well? How many hours a night do you sleep?

VOCABULARY PRACTICE

1. A person who is *listless* has very little (energy, money, breath, pressure).
2. To *put one's finger on* something is to (press it, identify it, ring it, accuse it).
3. To *pant* is to (walk, lift, smoke, breathe rapidly).
4. Which of the following activities does not constitute exercise? (walking, swimming, smoking, running)
5. A person who is *run-down* can be said to be (healthy, in poor physical condition, surprised, serious).
6. Someone who smokes two packs a day smokes (10, 20, 30, 40) cigarettes each day.
7. A diet which is harmoniously proportioned is called (temporary, busy, full, balanced).
8. Which of these words does not rhyme with *strain?* (rein, deign, crane, drain, lien, Maine)
9. Rob says he is *up to* two packs a day. In the past, he probably smoked (less than two packs, more than two packs, exactly two packs, not at all).
10. To *get dizzy* is to (walk up stairs, exercise, feel light-headed, understand).

Use Each of These Phrases in a Sentence

to put one's finger on • to seem to have • used to be • even more than • to carry around • to have the time • to take . . . off

Ford Motor Company

Buying a New Car

CUSTOMER: I'm interested in seeing the new mid-sized car you've been advertising. I forget the name, but it's the one that's supposed to be a "family car."

DEALER: It's right this way. The model you're referring to is the "Command"—one of our most popular cars this season. We only have a few left on the lot. Let's go out and take a look. Will you be trading in your present car?

CUSTOMER: Yes. It's the compact sedan parked in front of the showroom—the dark blue one.

DEALER: To save some time later, why don't I ask our estimator to have a look at your old car. He could drive it around the block, look it over, and tell us how much we might allow you on a trade-in.

CUSTOMER: You have a person who just makes estimates?

DEALER: That's all he does. Do you want him to check out your car?

CUSTOMER: Why not? Here are the keys. It's only five years old, and I've taken excellent care of it. Of course, there is that dent in the roof.

DEALER: A dent in the roof?

CUSTOMER: Just a little one.

DEALER: How did that happen?

CUSTOMER: A garage door closed on the car while I was driving out. I have an automatic door opener and it malfunctioned. I never got it fixed because it didn't affect the running of the car.

DEALER: Here we are. This baby will get you the best gas mileage of any car in its class. If you are still partial to dark colors, we can order one of these for you. As you can see, this one is fairly light.

CUSTOMER: No, I like this color. I might be ready for a change. What special features does it have?

DEALER: Factory-installed air conditioning, vinyl seat covers, and an AM-FM radio are standard equipment on all "Commands." Items like tinted glass, undercoating, cloth seat covers, and others are optional. Our factories are working around the clock to keep up with orders on this baby.

CUSTOMER: It looks like a heavy car, and yet you say it's economical to run?

DEALER: It uses lighter material in the body and frame, it has a new type of carburetor which cuts down on gas consumption, and the new emission controls allow you to use lower-cost gasoline. All in all, the

"Command" is one of the better cars on the road. Let's take a test drive so you can see how it handles. The power steering and power brakes on this car are great.

CUSTOMER: *(They get in.)* What's this knob for?

DEALER: That's to turn your secondary trip odometer back to zero. Your regular odometer measures the mileage your car goes during its lifetime. This one can be reset so you can measure shorter trips.

CUSTOMER: And what's this?

DEALER: That raises the antenna for the radio.

CUSTOMER: What if I wanted a manual transmission—stick shift?

DEALER: No, I'm sorry. The "Command" doesn't come with stick shift. If you wanted to have a three-speed, manual transmission, you'd have to get one of the economy-sized beauties. They're also great cars, but they're not as large—not as roomy. It depends on your family's needs. All of our mid- and large-sized cars come with automatic transmission these days.

CUSTOMER: Well, I like the car. It's a dream to drive. Let's go back to your office and see what kind of a deal you can give me. Then, I'll talk it over with my family. We need a new car, but we also have to stay within our budget.

COMPREHENSION AND CONVERSATION PRACTICE

1. Where does this dialogue take place? What people take part in the dialogue?
2. Can you tell the sexes of the people involved? Why/Why not?
3. What is the job of an estimator in a new car dealership?
4. What is a *carburetor?*
5. What kind of a car is a *sedan?*
6. Have you ever shopped for a new car? What was it like?
7. Did you think this car dealer was effective? Why/Why not?
8. How much would you expect to pay for a new mid-sized car? For an economy-sized car?
9. What are some options that are offered on new cars?
10. What does the term *gas mileage* mean?
11. How many miles (kilometers) are on your car's odometer?
12. What is the purpose of an *emission control?*
13. Give some examples of *compact* cars.
14. Do car models change frequently? Why/Why not?
15. What kind of new car would you like to buy if you could? Why?

VOCABULARY PRACTICE

1. An old or used car is often traded (in, off, to, over) for a new one.
2. When the salesperson refers to *this baby,* the *baby* is a (child, car, dent, model).
3. An *odometer* measures (gas consumption, speed, mileage, age).
4. To see how something responds to one's control is to see how it (looks, orders, buys, handles).
5. To *be partial to* something means to (want half, like it, hate it, eat it).
6. If a car is *a dream to drive,* it is (scary, dark, smooth, rough).
7. The opposite of *cut down on* is (cut up, test, increase, go out).
8. Give the past participle form of these verbs: forget, park, trade, take, drive, want, turn, measure, reset.
9. Working *around the clock* means working (aimlessly, with watches, only until noon, hard).

10. Any agreement or business transaction can be called a (budget, deal, economy, shift).

Use Each of These Phrases in a Sentence

to be interested in • right this way • in front of • to look something over • to affect the running • to be partial to • to be ready for a change • to cut down on • stick shift • to talk it over

unit (27)

Ford Motor Company

Getting a Tune-up

MS. PORTER: Good morning, Mr. Kobak. Here I am, as I promised. I brought my car in for a tune-up. I know I didn't make an appointment. Will you be able to take the car today?

MR. KOBAK: If you can leave it, we can, Ms. Porter. We usually operate on a first-come-first-serve basis. Would you like a major tune-up or a minor one?

MS. PORTER: From what you told me last week, I think I need a major one. You know—adjust the valves, change the points and spark plugs, change the motor oil, and lubricate it. If I need new air and oil filters, you'd better put them in too.

MR. KOBAK: Leave a phone number with us so we'll know how to reach you in case we find any problems. I'd want to notify you before I do something to your car that we haven't agreed on first.

MS. PORTER: Do you expect to find any problems?

MR. KOBAK: No, but there is so much hidden in a car's engine that we don't always know what we're going to find. I'll give you an example. We're going to set the timing in your car, and while we're doing it, we may find that your condenser is worn out. If it is, I'd recommend that you let us put a new one in.

MS. PORTER: So, you check over the entire car; is that right?

MR. KOBAK: That's right. We'll check to see that all the lights— both inside and out—are working properly. We'll check your tires to see that they're wearing evenly, and we'll rotate them if necessary. We'll check the fluid levels in all the areas where there is some sort of fluid.

MS. PORTER: I thought the only fluids were in the gas tank and in the motor.

MR. KOBAK: No, there's brake fluid, windshield washer fluid, transmission fluid, and a few others. You might even consider letting us flush out your radiator. I know I checked it last week, and it was fine, but it's not a bad idea to flush out the whole system once in a while and put in all new water and anti-freeze. It helps keep the cooling system clean.

MS. PORTER: I'm glad you're on the job, Mr. Kobak. I'm sure you'll do a good job, and I trust your judgment. By the way, Mr. Kobak, I've been thinking of trading in my car on a new one. After you do the tune-up, I'd like you to give me your overall impression of how the car is doing. What shape is it in?

MR. KOBAK: You mean you want me to advise you whether or not you should get a new car?

MS. PORTER: Yes. If you think that a lot of parts are going to wear out in the near future, I want to know about it. It may be that I would want to spend my money buying a new car rather than patching up an old one. As you can see, there are quite a few scrapes and dents on this one, and the paint is looking a little dull.

MR. KOBAK: I realize that your car will never win any beauty contests, Ms. Porter, but I can tell you right now, this is a solid car. It's in generally good shape, and I think it'll give you years more service. I've been working on this make of car for a long time, so I know what I'm talking about. I even bought one for my son. Do you know the Merrifield Paint & Body Shop out on the Boulevard?

MS. PORTER: I've passed it, but I've never been in there. Why?

MR. KOBAK: Old Pete Markovich out there will give you a good price on a new paint job. It'll look like new, and he'll even bang out those dents. Think it over. By the way, Ms. Porter, did you get that job you went to interview for last week?

MS. PORTER: Yes, I did, and if I don't catch my bus right now, I won't be keeping it for long. See you this afternoon, Mr. Kobak.

MR. KOBAK: Don't worry about your car, Ms. Porter. We'll take good care of it.

COMPREHENSION AND CONVERSATION PRACTICE

1. Where does this dialogue take place? What people take part in the dialogue?
2. What is the difference between a minor tune-up and a major one?
3. What general shape is the car in?
4. After a car has been driven a few thousand miles, what are some of the repairs and adjustments that have to be made?
5. What are *spark plugs?* Why do they have to be changed?
6. What are the functions of air and oil filters?
7. How much would you expect to pay for a major tune-up?
8. What lights are on the outside of a car? What lights are on the inside?
9. What does *rotating* tires mean? Why would you have it done?
10. What is a *beauty contest?* Explain the reference to a beauty contest in the dialogue.
11. What are some fluids a car needs?
12. Where do you (or your parents) take the family car for servicing?
13. Do you trust the judgment of the mechanic?
14. What are most car repair people like?
15. What do you think the inside of the place where Ms. Porter took her car looks like?

VOCABULARY PRACTICE

1. The opposite of *minor* is (major, small, insignificant, costly).
2. An *appointment* is a (part of a car, pen, time and place arrangement, tire).
3. To *agree* is to (pass, understand, give an example, concur).
4. If something *is worn out,* it (is outside, is like new, has become unusable, is a winter garment).
5. A *make* of car is a (manufacture, brand, style, year).
6. A strong gush of water is used to (tune up, rotate, patch, flush) a car's radiator.
7. The opposite of *dull* is (shiny, inactive, slow, depressed).

8. When something is *in good shape,* it is (angry, round, sad, not in need of repair).
9. A common synonym for *lubrication* is (oil, gas, fluid, grease).
10. To *check over* something is to (overlook it, examine it, reject it, enjoy it).

Use Each of These Phrases in a Sentence

as I promised • first-come-first-serve • to reach someone • in case • to give an example • to put in • to check over • not a bad idea • once in a while • on the job • the near future • to be in good shape • to look like new • to take good care of

unit (28)

Laimute E. Druskis

Investing Money

DAN: Hello, I'm Daniel McDonald. You must be Mr. and Mrs. Collings?

RICK: Yes, we are. Won't you come in, Mr. McDonald. And please call me Rick. This is my wife, Kate.

KATE: Good evening, Mr. McDonald. Let me take your coat. Would you like some coffee?

DAN: Yes, I would, thanks. You can call me Dan. Have you folks ever consulted an investment counselor before?

KATE: No, we haven't, Dan. It's only been in the past year or so that we've had enough money to be concerned with investing.

RICK: Kate had an aunt who died recently, and she left us a large sum of money in her will. We put it all in a simple savings account in our bank, but we know we can earn more than they're paying.

KATE: We've tried to investigate the various ways of investing money on our own, but there are so many conflicting claims that we got confused.

DAN: I'll see what I can do to make things a little clearer for you. First of all, let me say that there is no one, sure, "best" way to invest money. If there were, we'd all be doing it. There are several factors to consider. One is how involved you want to be in your investment.

RICK: What do you mean "involved"?

DAN: If you put your money in long-term bonds or securities, you know what the interest is going to be. It's usually a safe way to invest, but it's also passive. You just watch your money earn the same amount of interest year after year. On the other hand, if you invest in a precious metal, such as gold, you can get involved. When the price goes up, you can consider selling in order to make a profit. It's active involvement with your money. Do you see what I'm driving at?

KATE: I guess playing the stock market would be considered active involvement, wouldn't it?

DAN: Yes, it would. And "playing" is certainly the right word to use there, Kate. The stock market can provide people with a great deal of excitement, but it truly is a game. None of us really knows what's going to happen next in the market.

RICK: There are some safe stocks, though, aren't there? I've heard them called "blue chip" stocks.

DAN: Those are high-priced stocks in which the public

has a lot of confidence. Yes, they are fairly safe. They got their name from poker, you know.

RICK: No, I didn't know that. You mean the card game?

DAN: Yes. Many poker players use chips instead of money, and the highest valued chips are usually blue.

RICK: What about money market funds?

DAN: Money markets have been around since the early 1980s. Their interest rates vary from month to month, but they always seem to be a bit higher than savings accounts at banks or savings and loans. Have you considered real estate?

KATE: Land?

DAN: Not just land. Houses, vacation property, condominiums. The value of real property doesn't ever seem to go down. Of course, neighborhood events often determine a property's value, and it could lose value, but generally, the prices always go up.

KATE: I've always had an interest in managing property. I assume you mean that we would buy a house or apartment, or something, and then rent it to someone else.

DAN: Exactly. It's not only a generally sound investment, but you also get someone else to pay off the mortgage for you by paying you a fair rent. And, the tax advantages are good.

KATE: That sounds like the best route for me. What do you think, Rick?

RICK: I'd like to study these brochures Dan has brought

for us and consider all the possibilities before deciding.

DAN: A good idea. Keep this in mind while you're considering which route to take: It should be something you enjoy. There's no way to guarantee that your money will grow, so you might as well be doing something with it that brings you pleasure.

COMPREHENSION AND CONVERSATION PRACTICE

1. Where does this dialogue take place? What people take part in the dialogue?
2. If you had a lot of money to invest, what way might you choose?
3. What are *stocks?*
4. What are *blue chip* stocks? How did they get their name?
5. What's the difference between active and passive investment?
6. What's the difference between a commercial bank and a savings and loan association?
7. What is *interest?*
8. Give some examples of precious metals.
9. How much does gold sell for?
10. What are *money markets?* How much interest do they pay?
11. What is *real property?*
12. What is a *mortgage?* What are the mortgage rates in your area?
13. What is a *will?* Do you have one?
14. What do you think an investment counselor's job is?
15. What is the annual inflation rate in your area? How does inflation affect you?

VOCABULARY PRACTICE

1. To do something *on your own* means to do it (alone, with a lot of help, by buying it, by having possession of it).
2. If you *make things a little clearer,* you (lessen them, clarify them, polish them, manufacture them).

3. A share in a corporation is called a (bond, fund, stock, chip).
4. The opposite of a *profit* is a (sale, stock, interest, loss).
5. In the past year *or so* means in the past year (more or less, exactly, or not, if you wish).
6. Another term meaning *on the other hand* is (of course, however, after all, first of all).
7. If something has been *around* for ten years, it has been (circular, proven, in existence, safe) for ten years.
8. A *safe* investment is (a passive, an active, a real, a secure) one.
9. The *value* of an item is its (worth, cost, interest, security) to you.
10. Something that is *a bit* higher is (a great deal, slightly, not, rarely) higher.

Use Each of These Phrases in a Sentence

you must be • or so • on our own • I'll see what I can do • year after year • on the other hand • to drive at • a great deal of • the best route • which route to take • you might as well

Robert Sietsema

Borrowing Books from the Library

BORROWER: Good afternoon. I wonder if you could give me some information.

LIBRARIAN: I'd be happy to. What can I do for you?

BORROWER: I just moved out here to the suburbs from the city. I know the library systems are different, so I want to apply for a library card here.

LIBRARIAN: Certainly. Please fill out this card. Do you have any identification which shows your new address? I need to see something that verifies that you are a resident of the county.

BORROWER: *(He shows her some ID.)* How long will it take for me to get my new card?

LIBRARIAN: Not long. We'll process your application and mail you your new card in about a week. In the meantime, you can have this temporary card which you may use exactly as a regular card.

BORROWER: You mean I can use it today to borrow books?

LIBRARIAN: Yes. Are you familiar with our system?

BORROWER: Only if it's the same as the city's system. There we had what they called a card catalog. It was a big boxlike piece of furniture with lots of long drawers that had cards. Each card represents a different book. Is your system like that?

LIBRARIAN: No, ours is quite a bit different. Do you see those desk-top computer terminals over there? There are about a dozen of them throughout the library. We use them to locate our books. It's a system we introduced five years ago. We think it's more efficient than the old card catalog system. Come on. I'll show you how to use it.

BORROWER: I hope I don't have to have the skills of a computer programmer to be able to use it. All I want to do is borrow some books.

LIBRARIAN: It's easy. These small sheets of microfilm are called microfiche. That word comes from the French words for small index cards. You decide what book you want and pick the microfiche with that letter on it; it's all alphabetical. You can know the name of the book, the name of the author, or the subject—they're all lumped together on the same sheet.

BORROWER: That's handy.

LIBRARIAN: It's easy too. Let's try one as an example. Suppose you wanted to borrow *The Grapes of Wrath* by John Steinbeck. You could look under "G" for the title. We'll look on the "S" sheet for the author. Turn on the light, then move the microfilm, and . . . there it is! The "C" after the library code number tells you that it's here at the Central branch of the county library, rather than at one of our other branches. I'll give you a list of all the branches before you go.

BORROWER: My neighbor told me that I could borrow records here too. Is that right?

LIBRARIAN: Yes. We have a large record collection which we loan the same way we loan books. The selection is mostly of classical music. Over at this end of the library is our reference section. As with all library systems, these books may only be used here. No one is permitted to borrow them.

BORROWER: What about journals and magazines?

LIBRARIAN: Our periodicals section is quite complete. We subscribe to about 500 different weekly, monthly, and quarterly publications. We keep the current issues on display all along that far wall, and we keep back issues for a year. Issues prior to one year ago are on microfilm in the basement along with our technical textbook collection.

BORROWER: Today I just want to find a novel for some light reading. Where shall I look?

LIBRARIAN: These shelves right next to us have our latest acquisitions of fiction and nonfiction. The older fiction books are in alphabetical rows according to the author's last name. Stop by the desk on your way out to check out your books and to pick up a brochure describing all our services.

BORROWER: Thank you. I think I'll explore the whole library on my own in order to acquaint myself with all that you have.

LIBRARIAN: Be my guest!

COMPREHENSION AND CONVERSATION PRACTICE

1. Where does this dialogue take place? What people take part in the dialogue?
2. Describe the system of cataloging books in your library.
3. What ID (identification) does your library require in order to issue someone a card?
4. What is a *card catalog?*
5. What is *microfiche?* Where did that name come from?
6. What sheets of microfilm might you look on in order to find *Authentic Irish Recipes* by Juba Walsh?
7. What else besides books does a modern library lend?
8. What are the names of the last books you borrowed from the library?
9. Which periodicals does your library subscribe to?
10. Which periodicals do you subscribe to?
11. What does a library do with oversized books—those which are too large to fit on a normal shelf?
12. How is (or was) your school's library different from a public library?
13. What are the duties of a librarian?
14. What kinds of books are in the reference section of a library?
15. Who are your favorite authors?

VOCABULARY PRACTICE

1. Being *on display* means being (shown, hidden, playful, ashamed).
2. The area just outside a city's boundaries is called the (country, suburbs, downtown, region).
3. Which of the following is not a legal, political, and administrative subdivision within a country? (city, county, system, state)
4. Which verb phrase may be substituted for the italicized words? I am going to *lend you* a book. (borrow you, take you, give you, loan you)
5. To *locate* means to (find, lose, place on film, read).

6. Arrange these authors' names in alphabetical order: Hemingway, Wolfe, Shakespeare, Tolstoy, Dumas, Cervantes, Stowe, Vonnegut, Agee.
7. To put together in a single group is to (alphabetize, lump, pick, list).
8. Which of the following is not a definition of *branch?* (a limb of a tree, a local unit of a library system, a tributary of a river, a trademark)
9. To *acquaint* oneself is to make oneself (known, available, familiar with, select).
10. Give the noun forms of these verbs: acquire, describe, acquaint, display, subscribe, refer, identify, verify, apply, represent, locate, introduce.

Use Each of These Phrases in a Sentence

I wonder if you could • how long will it take • in the meantime • to be familiar with • quite a bit • to be able to • as with • to be permitted • prior to • according to

unit 30

United Nations

Meeting Teachers and Parents

MRS. MURPHY: Let's go to see Cindy's teacher first. The line outside his room looks shorter than any of the others.

MR. MURPHY: Okay. I suspect that the line is short because there's not much a second grade teacher can say to parents.

MR. WEISSMAN: *(After a few minutes' wait)* Come in, come in. You must be Mr. and Mrs. Murphy. Cindy is the only little girl in the class with red hair, and I can certainly see where she got it. My name is David Weissman.

MRS. MURPHY: How do you do, Mr. Weissman. You're right. Cindy is our daughter.

MR. WEISSMAN: You must be very proud of your little girl. She's very talented.

MR. MURPHY: Oh, she is? We see all the work she brings home. It all looks normal to us.

MR. WEISSMAN: Perhaps, but I put her work up on the wall to serve as an example to the others. Look over there. *(He shows them.)* This is her seat, by the way. Most of the parents like to see where their children sit.

MRS. MURPHY: I'm sure she doesn't sit there much, Mr. Weissman. At home, Cindy is always moving. I can never get her to sit still for one minute—not even during meals.

MR. WEISSMAN: I haven't had that problem with her. Many of the boys and girls are overly active, and I have some trouble getting them to stay at their places, but not Cindy. She even helps me with the other kids. Well, I hate to rush you, but I have dozens of other parents to meet tonight. Thanks for coming in. It was a pleasure meeting my best student's parents. Goodbye.

MRS. MURPHY: *(Walking down the hall to meet their seventh grade son's teacher)* I can't believe it. Was he talking about the same child we live with? Imagine that! She even helps the teacher! I can't get over it.

MR. MURPHY: I can't either, but I'm pleased to hear how well she's doing. Let's hope that Bill's teacher has equally good news.

MRS. MURPHY: Yes, I hope so. Say, this is running pretty smoothly tonight. I was glad that they told us about the possible school bus drivers' strike. It would be really difficult if there were a strike, but at least they have given us some time to prepare. Well, here we are at Ms. Kennedy's room.

MR. MURPHY: I'll bet we're going to like her. Bill speaks so highly of her. I don't believe he's ever taken to a teacher

the way he seems to be taking to her. *(They enter.)*
Good evening. Are you Elizabeth Kennedy?

MS. KENNEDY: Yes, I am.

MRS. MURPHY: We're the Murphys, Bill's parents.

MS. KENNEDY: Oh, yes. Please have a seat. We have a lot to talk about.

MR. MURPHY: We do?

MS. KENNEDY: Bill has probably told you how hard I've been coming down on him. I don't want you to get the wrong impression. It's not that I have anything against your son; it's just that I think he should be working harder. When the first report cards come out next week, Bill's grades are not going to be good.

MRS. MURPHY: Really, Ms. Kennedy? We didn't know he was doing poorly. What seems to be the difficulty?

MS. KENNEDY: He daydreams in class all the time instead of doing his assignments. I've spoken to his sixth grade teacher and looked over his record. He is a bright boy who is capable of doing excellent work, but he seems to be in a daze all the time in my class. I'm glad you're here so that we can talk about this problem. Do you have any ideas?

MR. MURPHY: Well, the only thing I can think of is that he's at an awkward age. His voice is changing, his arms and legs are growing longer and longer, and his complexion is getting worse.

MRS. MURPHY: Yes, now that I think about it, his manners at home aren't quite what they used to be. Is adolescence as difficult for all children?

MS. KENNEDY: Yes, it sure is. Well, that may be it. Bill's just coping with becoming a teenager. Maybe with your help and mine, he can weather this storm.

COMPREHENSION AND CONVERSATION PRACTICE

1. Where does this dialogue take place? What people take part in the dialogue?
2. What does the abbreviation *PTA* stand for? What similar organization is there in your school system? How are parent-teacher meetings conducted?
3. What did your teachers say about you when you were in the second grade? The seventh grade?
4. How do teachers use other students to help them with classroom problems?
5. What subjects are taught in the second grade?
6. Why do you think children often act differently in school from the way they act at home?
7. What did Mr. Weissman say about Cindy? How was she doing in school?
8. What did Ms. Kennedy say about Bill? How was he doing in school?
9. What is a *strike?*
10. Why might bus drivers go on strike?
11. What subjects are taught in the seventh grade?
12. What kinds of grades do (did) you get on your report cards?
13. Do you daydream often? What about?
14. At what age do boys' voices usually change?
15. Did you have trouble in school when you were a teenager?

VOCABULARY PRACTICE

1. People with red hair are called (redheads, redhairs, hairreds, reds).
2. To sit *still* means to sit (alone, without moving, noisily, active).
3. What is the difference between *Murphys* and *Murphy's?*

4. To run *smoothly* means to be (rough, flat, trouble-free, uneven).

5. Something that is about to occur is (general, terrible, informative, imminent).

6. To *talk about* something is to (talk around it, discuss it, belittle it, hide from it).

7. The difference between a *dream* and a *daydream* is that a daydream happens when a person is (awake, asleep, in school, in love).

8. To *come down on* means to (occur, recover, criticize or scold, enter).

9. To *weather a storm* means to (get wet, stay inside, be angry with, remain safe).

10. To *take to* someone or something is to (become fond of, remove, hire, get).

Use Each of These Phrases in a Sentence

to suspect that • you must be • how do you do • to sit still • to come in • to get over something • I'll bet that • to take to • to come down on • to have something against

unit (31)

BMW of North America

Learning to Drive

HILDA: Heidi, are you ready for your first driving lesson?

HEIDI: You bet I am! I can hardly wait!

(The two sisters get into their parents' car. Heidi is behind the wheel.)

HILDA: Okay, let's start with the basics. Make sure the arrow is pointing to "P" on that indicator behind the steering wheel. The automatic gear shift has to be in Park in order for the car to start.

HEIDI: What do the other letters stand for?

HILDA: "D" is for Drive, "N" is for Neutral, "R" is for Reverse, and the "L" is a special Low gear for going up steep hills or getting a lot of extra traction. You can shift gears by moving that lever on the steering wheel, but you should be stopped before changing gears. Okay. Let's fasten our safety belts and adjust the seat so you're comfortable and can see well.

HEIDI: My legs are a lot shorter than yours, so I'm going to have to move the seat up all the way. Which is the ignition key?

HILDA: The one with the rounded end. The one with the rectangular-shaped end unlocks the doors and the trunk. Turn the key to the right, and when you hear the engine start, let go of it. I remember when Dad was teaching me to drive, I held the key after the engine started, and I almost burned out the starter. Good! You did it! Let's let the engine warm up for a minute. In cold weather like this, it might take a while for the engine to get ready to go.

HEIDI: That sounds like me on mornings when I don't want to get up to go to school. What next?

HILDA: Look in the rearview mirror and the side view mirror to make sure that no one is coming. I always double-check by turning my head to look back too. Now you're ready. The gauge on the dashboard says the engine is warm. Put it into Drive. No cars coming? Good. Now slowly pull out into the street.

HEIDI: Where shall I drive?

HILDA: Let's drive over to Delaware Street and practice in the schoolyard. Since it's Saturday, no one will be there, so we'll have the whole place to ourselves. You can practice turning, parking, backing up—everything.

HEIDI: Oops! I guess I braked too hard. I saw that stop sign and wanted to be sure I stopped in time.

HILDA: These power brakes take some getting used to. It's okay, though. Don't get nervous. You just have to learn to ease your foot on the brake the same way you ease your foot on the accelerator when you want to go forward. Speaking of going forward, you're holding up traffic.

HEIDI: I think I'll turn right at the next corner, right?

HILDA: Right! No, I mean left. Turn left to get to the schoolyard. Put your turn signal on so the other cars will know what you're about to do. Even though you have the right of way because the light is green, you should still look carefully to see that no one is in your way before you make the turn.

HEIDI: How come Granddad points his finger out the window when he's going to turn?

HILDA: That's the old-fashioned way of signaling a turn before cars had flashing lights. Here we are at the school. Turn in here and pull over to the corner of the yard. Okay, put it into Park, put the emergency brake on, and turn off the ignition while we discuss what we'll practice.

HEIDI: How am I doing so far?

HILDA: Pretty good, but we need to talk about speed. The limit on normal city streets is twenty-five or thirty miles per hour. If you had noticed your speedometer on the last block, you'd have seen that you were doing forty. That's too fast for local travel. Your foot is a little heavy on both the brake and the gas pedals. Let's work on that problem first.

COMPREHENSION AND CONVERSATION PRACTICE

1. Where does this dialogue take place? What people take part in the dialogue?
2. Do you know how to drive? Who taught (will teach) you?
3. Do you think it would be difficult to teach someone to drive?
4. What other letters or numbers might appear on a gear indicator?
5. What is the function of safety belts? Do you wear one?
6. How many mirrors does a car normally have?
7. What do the keys to your car look like?
8. What should a driver do before backing up?
9. What does a stop sign look like? What color and shape do other street signs have?
10. What are the colors of a street light? What do they signify?
11. What are the various pedals under the driver's feet called?
12. What is the *right of way*?
13. What is an *emergency* brake? How is it different from a car's regular brakes?
14. What is the speed limit on the street where you live?
15. Make a list of what you consider to be the most important things a person who is learning to drive should know.

VOCABULARY PRACTICE

1. The phrase *you bet I am* means (I certainly am, I'll make a bet with you, the wager is good, I'm not ready).
2. The part of a car which has the speedometer, the odometer, the fuel gauge, etc., is called the (turn signal, dashboard, accelerator, brake).
3. A car can back up when the gear arrow indicates ("P," "D," "R," "N").
4. An engine which is running may be said to be (in gear, burned out, adjusted, warming up).
5. To *hold up* traffic means to (delay it, start it, pull out of it, turn it).
6. Another name for the *accelerator* is the (brake, gas pedal, gear, turn signal).

7. To *pull out into* means to (brake, stop, drive, signal).
8. *Even though* means (because, the same way, you bet, despite the fact that).
9. A driver who is *doing forty* is (going 40 mph, stopped, driving within the speed limit at all times, parking).
10. *How come* means (come this way, why, in what way, greetings).

Use Each of These Phrases in a Sentence

you bet • hardly wait • behind the wheel • to stand for • to shift gears • to back up • how come • to warm up • to make sure • to pull out • in time • to get used to • to go forward • to hold up traffic • right of way • to make a turn • to work on

unit (32)

National Center for Atmospheric Research
National Science Foundation/David Baumhefner

Talking about the Weather

NORA: It says in the newspaper that the temperature will be in the mid-eighties in Key West today. No rain is expected, and the forecast says the temperature won't go below seventy-five for the next week or so.

NICK: Are you hinting at a Florida vacation, my dear?

NORA: I sure am.

NICK: But I enjoy this cold weather. It's refreshing after that hot, muggy summer we had.

NORA: It was a terribly hot summer, I agree. Do you remember the day our air conditioner broke down? There was ninety percent humidity and the temperature stayed above one hundred for four straight days. There wasn't a breeze anywhere. But that's not what it's like in the Keys. There are balmy Caribbean winds blowing every day.

NICK: What's wrong with a few low temperatures? It

makes living here in Michigan interesting. If it were sunny and warm all the time, we wouldn't have the dramatic changes of season.

NORA: I confess that I do like the fall. The brilliant colors of the leaves when they change and blow in the wind are breathtaking. Autumn is always beautiful in this part of the country. If only it weren't followed by winter. . . .

NICK: I know what you're going to say about the snow, but surely you see the beauty in snow too. Just look at that carpet of white out there on our lawn. It's a winter wonderland!

NORA: It's freezing!

NICK: But it's beautiful.

NORA: The temperature hasn't gotten above twenty degrees for three weeks, and it's supposed to go below zero again tonight. The sidewalks are slick with ice, and we have to shovel the snow off the steps every other day. That's not beautiful!

NICK: I don't mind the extra work. For me, it's worth it to be able to experience the brisk air and to take part in the winter sports. You know how I love sledding, skiiing, and ice-skating!

NORA: I know, and I'm glad you're having fun. It's just that I'm tired of being cold. I wish spring were here. I look forward to the soft, gentle rains and the flowers. I want to see green on the trees instead of white. I want to be able to go outside without putting on several layers of clothing just to be comfortable.

NICK: Well, I agree that winter does seem awfully long when we get to January.

NORA: It seemed long to me in November!

NICK: This constant cloudiness is what gets me down. Last night on the news, the meteorologist said it would be partly cloudy for the rest of the week. That sky doesn't look partly cloudy to me. There's not a trace of sun or blue.

NORA: It looks like another storm is coming too.

NICK: Yes, the sky over there in the west is getting dark.

NORA: I'll bet it's going to snow again tonight.

NICK: Yes, the winds are already beginning to blow hard.

NORA: The sky would be clear from sunup to sundown in Florida. The winds would be warm and tropical. No heavy winter clothes. No slipping on the ice. No. . . .

NICK: Okay, you've talked me into it. Let's get out our bathing suits and suntan oil and put away our snow shovels. Let's go south.

COMPREHENSION AND CONVERSATION PRACTICE

1. Where does this dialogue take place? What people take part in the dialogue?
2. Do you think the two people are married? How old do you think they are?
3. Which is your favorite season? Why?
4. Which winter sports do you enjoy? Which would you like to try?
5. What are some advantages of living in a cold climate? Some disadvantages?
6. What are the signs of the coming of spring?
7. What happens in nature in the fall?

8. Using Fahrenheit temperatures, as the people in the dialogue do, tell the temperature today. What was the coldest temperature you remember? The hottest?
9. What is a *meteorologist?* What is his or her function?
10. What is the weather like in January where you live? In May? In August? In October?
11. What is the difference between *heat* and *humidity?*
12. Why do people have to shovel their walks after a snowfall?
13. What are the predominant colors of each of the four seasons?
14. Have you ever gone on vacation in order to get to (or escape from) a specific weather situation?
15. What's today's weather forecast?

VOCABULARY PRACTICE

1. At which of the following temperatures will water freeze? (20°, 33°, 75°, 80° Fahrenheit)
2. To *hint* is to (imply or suggest, expect, tell, enjoy).
3. When the air is warm and extremely humid, it is said to be (cloudy, muggy, chilly, breezy).
4. A *balmy* breeze is (stormy, snowy, mild and pleasant, crazy).
5. Another name for *fall* is (spring, summer, winter, autumn).
6. Which of the following temperature changes involves *dropping below zero?* (80° to 50°, 75° to 32°, 20° to 0°, 20° to −10°)
7. Which of the following is *not* a winter sport in Michigan? (swimming, skiing, sledding, ice-skating)
8. What color is the sky on a cloudless day? (grey, blue, white, dark, green)
9. What are the four main directions on a compass?
10. Solid white precipitation is called (rain, humidity, snow, clouds).

Use Each of These Phrases in a Sentence
to be expected • to break down • to get above (a temperature) • it makes • if only • to go below (a temperature) • not a trace • from sunup to sundown • to talk someone into something

unit (33)

United Nations

Flying to Los Angeles

JIM: There seems to be some delay. Our plane is sup-posed to leave at 2:10, and it's already 2:20. Wait. That's our flight they're announcing over the loud-speaker now. Flight 620—now boarding for Los Angeles, Gate 14.

BOB: Where did I put my boarding pass?

JIM: It's right there in your pocket. Don't worry. We're checked in. We've got our seats in the No Smoking section. It's going to be a very pleasant flight.

BOB: I'm a little nervous. I've never flown before. What if I get sick?

JIM: There's nothing at all to worry about. Once you're up in the air, it's just like sitting at home in your own living room.

BOB: That's just where I'd like to be right now—sitting at home in my own living room.

ATTENDANT: *(Jim and Bob board the plane, store their hand luggage, and sit in their assigned seats. The flight attendant passes through the aisle as the plane prepares to take off.)* Fasten your seat belts, please. Welcome to Flight 620 now departing for Los Angeles. We will arrive at 4:47 local time, and we'll be flying at an altitude of thirty-five thousand feet.

BOB: What's the idea of the seat belts?

JIM: You're supposed to fasten yourself firmly to your seat in case of an accident. Otherwise you may be thrown against the seat in front and injured.

BOB: And if the plane catches fire, I won't be able to get out either.

JIM: Nothing like that ever happens. You're beginning to make me nervous.

BOB: What's that terrible noise?

JIM: Those are the engines. They're warming them up. We're about to take off. Look! We're starting. Isn't it thrilling? Now we're leaving the ground. Bob, stop clenching your teeth and open your eyes. We're already in the air, and you're completely safe and sound. Look down below and see how New York looks from the air.

BOB: Maybe I'll get sick if I look down. Good grief, what was that? The plane dropped suddenly.

JIM: That was probably an air pocket. Every time a plane hits an air pocket, it always dips a little.

BOB: Now my ear hurts. It just popped terribly. I suppose that's the atmospheric pressure. How high are we? I have heard that if you open your mouth and swallow hard, your ears won't pop. (*Between swallows*) How many different things can happen to you in an airplane?

JIM: Nothing serious is going to happen to you. Thousands of people travel by plane every day and nothing happens to them. Be a little philosophical. When your turn comes to die, you'll die—and not before.

BOB: But suppose today happens to be the pilot's turn?

JIM: Then the copilot will take over. These big planes always carry two pilots. Now please sit back and relax. We'll soon be in Los Angeles, and all your troubles will be over.

BOB: I wish I had taken out some of that flight insurance I saw advertised in the airport.

JIM: I wish you hadn't seen that airplane disaster movie last night. That wasn't very smart. Believe me, Bob, it's safer flying in this jumbo jet than it is crossing the street in Manhattan. Now settle back. The flight attendants will bring our meals soon, and we can watch the in-flight movie.

COMPREHENSION AND CONVERSATION PRACTICE

1. Where does this dialogue take place? What people take part in the dialogue?
2. To what city are the two friends going? From what city are they coming?
3. Why is Bob nervous?
4. What was your first flight like? Were you nervous?
5. Do you fly often? Where?
6. How does the cost of travel by plane compare with travel by other means of transportation?

7. How long do you think it takes to fly from New York to Los Angeles? From your hometown to Los Angeles? How much would these flights cost?
8. What are the duties of a flight attendant?
9. What does *take off* mean in airline language?
10. What is an *air pocket*? How do air pockets affect planes?
11. Why do you think some people feel sick when they fly?
12. Which airlines do you think are the best?
13. Why do planes fly so high (35,000 feet is over 64 miles or almost 11 kilometers up)? What is the air like at that height?
14. What airplane disaster movies have you seen?
15. Why do some people's ears pop when they fly?

VOCABULARY PRACTICE

1. A *loudspeaker* is (a boring person, one with a bass voice, an instrument for increasing the volume of the voice).
2. A *gate* is a (delayed flight, means of entrance, small animal, frightened passenger).
3. To *board* a plane is to (leave it, enjoy plane travel, inspect it, get on it).
4. The word *worry* rhymes with (merry, hurry, fairy, diary).
5. When a plane *takes off*, it (dips, leaves the ground, arrives on schedule, is delayed).
6. The opposite of to *take off* is to (land, start, come, have motor trouble).
7. A synonym for *in case of* is (because, on account of, in the event of, in order to).
8. A synonym for *terrible* is (kindly, dreadful, amusing, bitter).
9. If you *are about to* do something, that means that you (are hesitant about doing it, have just done it, have to do it, are on the point of doing it).
10. To *take over* something is to (inspect it, reject it, fall over it, assume control of it).

Use Each of These Phrases in a Sentence
to be supposed to • to check in • what's the idea of • in case of • to make someone nervous • safe and sound • Good grief! • to hit an air pocket • to pop (one's ears) • believe me • to settle back

unit (34)

Rick Maiman

Applying for a Job

MR. WILSON: Sit down, please, Ms. Sloan. We have your letter and resume in answer to our ad in the paper. I'd like to talk with you about your qualifications for the position.

MS. SLOAN: *(She takes a seat.)* I suppose you have received a great many replies to your advertisement, Mr. Wilson.

MR. WILSON: I haven't counted the exact number of replies, but I would say that there were at least fifty. Naturally, many who applied don't have the qualifications we require, but we have picked out the ten or twelve best replies for interviews. Your letter was among the ten or twelve we picked out.

MS. SLOAN: It's good to know my letter was acceptable. It's sometimes difficult to answer a newspaper advertisement well.

MR. WILSON: I would say that your letter was one of the best we received. I am always amazed at the poor letters some people write when applying for a job. They write illegibly in longhand and include many personal facts which are not important. At the same time, they fail to state simply and clearly their qualifications for the job. Incidentally, you mentioned in your letter that you had already done considerable work in selling.

MS. SLOAN: I was a field representative for five years for a large commercial school. I enrolled new students for the school.

MR. WILSON: What did your work consist of exactly?

MS. SLOAN: The school supplied me with leads which were generally simply the names of prospective students who had telephoned or written to the school requesting information. I had to visit these students in their homes, talk with their parents, and so forth.

MR. WILSON: This job for which we are interviewing applicants is somewhat similar—except, of course, you would be selling typewriters rather than commercial courses. We pay two hundred fifty dollars a week plus a ten-percent commission on all sales. Your school experience would be very useful, since in this job you would also call on schools and colleges. You would visit typing classes, demonstrate new machines, and talk with school officials and commercial teachers in an effort to interest them in buying our typewriters. The job occasionally involves some traveling.

MS. SLOAN: I am prepared to travel if necessary. As I said in my letter, I have my own car.

MR. WILSON: That's important. We give you an allowance for all automobile and traveling expenses.

MS. SLOAN: I'm sure that I could do the work. I feel that I have the necessary qualifications.

MR. WILSON: Frankly, Ms. Sloan, I was very impressed by your letter and talking to you has reinforced that good impression. However, we naturally want to interview the other applicants before we make any final decision.

MS. SLOAN: I included the names of several references in my letter. I can also send you copies of personal recommendations from my last two employers.

MR. WILSON: I'd like that. Please send them. I'm interested to see what kind of a worker your bosses thought you were. If we decided to hire you, when could you start?

MS. SLOAN: I could start almost immediately. I would like to give my present employer a week or ten days' notice, but otherwise I would be free to begin any time.

MR. WILSON: That's fine. *(He rises to indicate end of interview.)* You'll hear from us soon, one way or the other. As soon as we have interviewed the remainder of the applicants, we will make our final decision. We will telephone you. It has been a pleasure to talk with you.

MS. SLOAN: Thank you, sir! I hope to hear from you.

COMPREHENSION AND CONVERSATION PRACTICE

1. Where does this dialogue take place? What people take part in the dialogue?
2. What ad did Ms. Sloan answer?
3. What did the personnel manager think of most people's letter-writing ability?
4. What are some of the components of a good application letter? Of a resume?
5. Have you written many letters applying for jobs? What were they like?
6. What was Ms. Sloan's previous experience?
7. What was the job she was applying for?
8. How much did the job pay?
9. Why didn't the personnel manager hire Ms. Sloan immediately? Do you think he will eventually?
10. Why did the personnel manager want further references?
11. What is an *automobile* or *travel allowance?* How much is it usually?
12. What is a *commission?*
13. Would you like a job such as the one Ms. Sloan is applying for? Why/Why not?
14. Do you think you would be a good salesperson? What would you like to sell?
15. Describe your last job interview.

VOCABULARY PRACTICE

1. A *reply* is an (interview, answer, application, advertisement).
2. To *pick out* means to (retire, apply, review, select).
3. Handwriting which cannot be read is said to be (edible, inedible, legible, illegible).
4. *Amazed* means (pleased, amused, greatly surprised, annoyed).
5. A *prospective* student is one who is (good, rejected, expected, angry).
6. The opposite of *public* is (private, well-to-do, shy, awkward).
7. What is the noun form of these verbs? (demonstrate, enroll, qualify, accept, prepare, suppose)

8. *Frankly* means (quickly, honestly and openly, energetically, slyly).
9. *One way or the other* means (affirmative, north and south, either affirmative or negative, quickly).
10. That which is left over is called the (remainder, indication, notice, resume).

Use Each of These Phrases in a Sentence

in answer to • at least • to pick out • incidentally • to consist of • and so forth • to call on • one way or the other • but otherwise • it has been a pleasure

Laimute E. Druskis

Watching TV

CARL: Welcome home from work, Penny. I'm glad to see you.

PENNY: How are you feeling, Carl?

CARL: Much better, thanks. I've rested all day, with only the television as my companion. In fact, all this week, since I've been sick, all I seem to have the energy to do is watch TV.

PENNY: What did you watch today?

CARL: I started with some game shows this morning. I love to try to answer the questions along with the contestants. I won ten thousand dollars today.

PENNY: You did! How wonderful! How?

CARL: No, no, not really. I mean, if I had been a contestant in the studio in California or wherever they tape the show, I would have won that much. I answered almost all the questions correctly.

PENNY: Oh. Well, it cheered you up anyway, didn't it? What did you watch next?

CARL: At 1:00 I switched to the cable channel and watched a movie with Jane Fonda and Burt Reynolds. It was terrific. I really like both of them, and they acted well together. The great part about some cable networks is that there are no commercial interruptions.

PENNY: I'm glad it's available in our neighborhood. I like it too. Didn't I read that there was an old Humphrey Bogart movie on this afternoon? I thought you liked him.

CARL: I do, but I had already watched enough TV by the time it came on. I mean, I'll still watch more, but I guess my eyes were tired because I lay down and took a nap just before it came on. When I awoke, it was over, so I watched the news on Channel 11.

PENNY: Anything important happen?

CARL: The bank at the corner of Broad and Market was robbed this afternoon. They had a reporter on the scene who was covering the event live. It was very exciting. She interviewed tellers who were in the bank when the gunman took the money. The live coverage made the news seem lifelike.

PENNY: Is there anything good on tonight?

CARL: That new detective show has been getting good reviews. I haven't seen it yet, but I think it might be good. I'd like to watch it. What about you? Now that you're here, we should decide together what to watch. Is there anything on that you'd like to see?

PENNY: Yes, there's that sitcom that I watch every week—
you know, the one which is set in a downtown hotel.
It's been on the air for years, but I never get tired
of the humor on that show. I guess situation come-
dies are one type of show that the public never
gets enough of. I love the characters and the way
they interact with the guests at the hotel.

CARL: When is it on?

PENNY: At 9:00 on Channel 5.

CARL: Oh, darn! That's when the Public Broadcasting network is having that show about the animals of the
Andes. The focus is on condors, but it covers all
types of creatures from insects to llamas.

PENNY: Let's see if that show is going to be repeated at a
later date so you can see it. Where is the Sunday
newspaper TV guide? Here it is. You're in luck.
That show will be on another educational channel
the day after tomorrow.

CARL: Good. Now we can both watch your show and
enjoy it. By the way, the late-night talk show tonight
promises to be good. I read in the previews section
of this morning's paper that some of our favorite
actors and actresses are going to be on at 11:30
with a surprise host. I look forward to it—if I can
stay awake that long.

PENNY: I'll bet you can. You're becoming such a television
watcher that I'm sure you can stay up until the late,
late show.

CARL: You're right. It's getting so that I only know to go to
bed when I hear the national anthem.

COMPREHENSION AND CONVERSATION PRACTICE

1. Where does this dialogue take place? What people take part in the dialogue?
2. When does Carl start watching TV every day? When does he stop?
3. What kinds of questions do game show hosts ask their contestants?
4. What is *cable TV?*
5. What kinds of movies are shown on TV in your area?
6. Do you watch news shows? Which ones?
7. Do you enjoy watching TV? What kinds of shows do you like best?
8. What is your favorite program?
9. What kinds of events do TV news shows cover live?
10. What is the value of live TV?
11. Which are the most popular shows in your area?
12. What is a *sitcom?* Why do you think sitcoms are popular?
13. What are *reviews?* Who gives them? How?
14. How do most television stations end their programming day?
15. What are *talk shows?* Do you ever watch them?

VOCABULARY PRACTICE

1. The vowel sound in *guide* is pronounced the same as the vowel sound in (side, ruin, quiz, lieu).
2. A person who competes is called a (host, contestant, detective, teller).
3. Give the past tense of the following verbs: watch, awaken, win, read, switch, rob, give, stay up.
4. A *gunman* is a person who (sells guns, works in a bank, uses a gun in a crime, covers crimes for TV news).
5. All of the following, except one, describe something being shown on television: on, on the air, televised, viewed.
6. If something *cheers you up,* you are (happy, sad, colorful, silly).
7. A *nap* is a (TV show, short sleep, long night's sleep, snack).
8. The extent of reporting and analysis of the news is called (show business, sitcom, coverage, network).

9. In TV terms, the opposite of *live* is (dead, asleep, on the air, taped).

10. Another way of saying *in luck* is (lucky, luckless, with luck, by luck).

Use Each of These Phrases in a Sentence

welcome home • along with • not really • to cheer someone up • to come on (the TV) • to be over • to cover • real life • on the air • to get enough of • oh, darn • to stay awake • to stay up

unit ⑥36

Robert Siersema

Driving to a Shopping Center

CHRIS: Does anyone want to go with me? The Nieman-Marcus department store chain has just opened a branch at the new shopping mall, and they're having a big celebration for their grand opening. The first fifteen hundred customers get a free T-shirt. I want to be there in time to get mine. Who wants to go?

MARY: I do! I've been reading about that mall. It's supposed to be the largest in the state. I forget the statistics on the size, but their parking lot is larger than the one at the football stadium. It should accommodate thousands of cars.

KAYE: I do too. I hear that they have some wonderful specialty shops in the new shopping center. I want to go to the new chocolate shop. I know it's going to be expensive, but I have such a weakness for chocolate that I can't resist a whole store which is dedicated to it.

MARY: Shopping centers like that one always have plenty of shoe stores, so I think I'll look for some new shoes to wear to Eva's party tonight. Let's go!

CHRIS: *(They drive to the shopping center.)* Look at this traffic! It's amazing that so many people had the same idea at the same time.

KAYE: You did say they were giving away free prizes. Maybe everyone wants a T-shirt. This traffic is heavy, but it's moving nicely. They've designed the entrances to the mall well. Look, there's even an underground parking area. That would be handy for cold weather and for when it rains. Let's find a parking space and go in. I'm getting anxious.

MARY: Me too. *(They park and walk to the entrance to the center.)* Here's a map of the entire mall listing all the stores, the various entrances, the rest rooms, and the services available. I think I'll take the escalator to the lower level and go to the cosmetics store first. I hear that they let customers try on different shades of eye shadow and mascara. I need some makeup.

CHRIS: I'm headed for Nieman-Marcus, but I may stop at the health food store before I get there. I want to compare their prices with the store in the shopping center we usually go to.

MARY: I'm going to look for shoes. This directory says there are about a dozen shoe stores in the mall. What fun! I'll be here all morning. However, I think I'll stop for a cup of coffee before I begin.

CHRIS: It says here you have to go to the top floor to get it. We have to take the escalator to get there.

KAYE: Okay. There's the escalator, by the waterfall.

MARY: Okay. Since we all have different ideas and different goals here, we'd better plan to meet later. We'll
never find each other in this crowd if we don't pick
a time and place to meet.

CHRIS: Good idea. I suggest we meet at the fountain at the
entrance to Fashion Court. I haven't seen it, but
according to the map we all looked at, it seems
easy to find. Let's split up and meet there in two
hours.

KAYE: Is that enough time for you to do your shoe shopping?

MARY: It is if I don't get sidetracked by some of the other
stores. I saw that the bookstore was having a grand
opening sale. You know me in bookstores; you
know how I lose track of time.

CHRIS: If we don't see you at the fountain in two hours,
we'll know where to look for you. I'll see you later.
I'm going to ride back down to the health food
store. I'll skip coffee.

COMPREHENSION AND CONVERSATION PRACTICE

1. Where does this dialogue take place? What people take part in
   the dialogue?
2. What kinds of stores did they expect to find at the shopping
   center?
3. What kinds of stores are at shopping centers near you?
4. What are some examples of specialty shops?
5. What is the difference between an *escalator* and an *elevator*?
6. What is the purpose of levels in a mall?

7. Where is the largest parking lot in your area? How many cars does it hold?
8. Where do you do most of your shopping?
9. What are the advantages of shopping at a shopping center? The disadvantages?
10. Is the merchandise the same in shopping center stores as in regular stores? What about the prices?
11. What happens at a shopping center when a child gets separated from his or her parents?
12. What's the largest mall you have ever been to? How many stores did it have?
13. Why would there be a waterfall in a shopping mall?
14. What types of products are sold in health food stores?
15. What were the main shopping interests of the three people in the dialogue?

VOCABULARY PRACTICE

1. Explain the differences in meaning among these three words which all sound alike: *there, their, they're.*
2. Explain the difference in emphasis between "You said you wanted to go" and "You did say you wanted to go."
3. Another term for *rest room* is (fountain, bathroom, store, mall).
4. Which of the following items would not be found in a cosmetics store? (eye shadow, mascara, shoes, lipstick, rouge)
5. Note the difference in pronunciation between these sets of words: makeup (noun) and make up (verb); complex (adjective) and complex (noun); record (noun) and record (verb).
6. The collection of numerical data is called (statistics, celebration, traffic, elegance).
7. To *split up* is to (rejoin, separate, go to a sale, meet later).
8. To *head for* means to (play soccer, stand erect, wear a hat, aim in a certain direction).
9. A person who has *a weakness for* chocolate (hates, loves, is indifferent to, can't stand) it.
10. A person who *loses track of time* is usually (early, on time, late, punctual).

Use Each of These Phrases in a Sentence

to head for • to be supposed to be • me too • lower level • to stop at • to look for • to look like • one of the most. . . • to split up • to get sidetracked • to lose track of • I'll see you later

Robert Sietsema

Buying Greeting Cards

CLERK:	May I help you?
CUSTOMER:	Yes. Next week is my cousin's birthday, and I want to send her a birthday card. Do you have a large selection?
CLERK:	Yes, we do. This section in the front of the store has only holiday greeting cards, as you can see, but we have cards for all occasions in the aisles farther back. Call me if you need any assistance.
CUSTOMER:	Thank you. I will. *(He starts to walk to the rear of the store, but a card display catches his eye.)* I'm surprised that you have Christmas cards out so early. It's only the middle of October.
CLERK:	Some people like to buy and write their cards early, and the post office advises us every year to send our holiday cards as early as possible. They

must have to handle millions of pieces of mail in December because of all the Hanukkah and Christmas cards people send.

CUSTOMER: These look attractive. I like the simple design and the simple message: "Season's Greetings." I see here that you engrave the cards at a nominal cost. How much is "nominal"?

CLERK: That depends on how many you order. The rate is based on volume, so the more you order to be printed, the less it costs you per card. It also depends on how many lines you want. Most people just have their names printed, but some have several lines of print.

CUSTOMER: I'll think it over while I'm looking for the birthday card. *(He chooses several cards and returns to the store clerk.)* I'm having a hard time deciding which of these cards to send her. This one is funny to me, but I don't know if she has the same sense of humor. This second one is pretty, but it's not representative of me; it doesn't have any of my personality or taste in it. This third one is my favorite, but it doesn't have a poem or message inside as the others do.

CLERK: That's one of our personal message cards. It's designed that way intentionally so that the sender can write a message of his or her choice.

CUSTOMER: I'm not feeling very creative. Perhaps I should keep looking.

CLERK: I'll help you. What about this one? The message is warm and friendly, and it even uses the phrase "favorite relative" on the cover. Do you like this one?

CUSTOMER: That's perfect. I'll take it. Thanks so much for helping me. I guess you know all the cards in the shop, don't you?

CLERK: Not all of them, but almost all. While you're here, why don't you look over our selection of cards for other occasions. If you're like most people, you don't keep cards around the house for those times which come upon us unexpectedly.

CUSTOMER: I noticed that you had a few rows of sympathy cards on this rack. I have needed them in the past, and it's been a nuisance to run out to the store to buy one. Maybe you're right. Maybe I should stock up on cards like that.

CLERK: We also have get well cards, graduation cards, friendship cards, even retirement cards. You may have noticed that greeting cards have become very specialized. There probably isn't an occasion that we don't have a card for—marriage, confirmation, new baby, anniversary, thank you, change of address—you name it.

CUSTOMER: I noticed too that the birthday cards were specific. There was one, "To My Niece and Her Husband." I'd never seen one that specific before.

CLERK: The world is full of specialization. Keep us in mind too when you want to send cards for special holidays. We stock a large line of cards for Valentine's Day, St. Patrick's Day, Easter—all the major holidays.

CUSTOMER: I'll keep that in mind. You may turn me into a greeting card sender. For now, however, I'll just buy this birthday card which you helped me choose. Thanks for all your help.

COMPREHENSION AND CONVERSATION PRACTICE

1. Where does this dialogue take place? When? What people take part in the dialogue?
2. Why did the customer want to send a card?
3. Do you send holiday cards in December? How many?
4. What other times would you send greeting cards?
5. Do you send cards for friends' and relatives' birthdays?
6. What type of birthday card do you usually send?
7. What type of birthday card do you most like to receive?
8. When was the last time you received a greeting card?
9. Why might someone send a sympathy card? A get well card?
10. Which relatives do you send birthday cards to?
11. What and when are the three holidays mentioned in the dialogue, namely, Valentine's Day, St. Patrick's Day, and Easter?
12. What is a *sense of humor*? Do most people have the same sense of humor?
13. What sort of message would you write on a personal message card (one that had no preprinted poem or message inside)?
14. What else besides greeting cards might you find in a card shop?
15. What is the main idea in sending a greeting card?

VOCABULARY PRACTICE

1. To *keep something in mind* is to (forget it, borrow it, look at it, remember it).
2. To *stock up on* cards is to (provide a supply, keep farm animals, send birthday cards, keep away).
3. Each of the following is a relative except one: aunt, niece, clerk, cousin.
4. Something that *catches your eye* (repels you, attracts you, falls on you, gets into your eye).
5. A *nominal* fee is a (minimal, large, costly, expensive) one.
6. The *ui* vowel sound in *nuisance* is pronounced like the vowel sound in (quiz, you, ruin, buzz).
7. To *reflect on* something or to ponder it is to think it (over, off, on, under).

8. The opposite of a *major* holiday is a (big, important, minor, simple) one.
9. What is the difference between *running out* to the store to buy something and *running out* of paper when you've used it all?
10. A *rack* is a frame used to (send, write, handle, display) items such as greeting cards.

Use Each of These Phrases in a Sentence

a large selection • all occasions • to catch one's eye • so early • to handle • that depends on • to think something over • to keep looking • almost all • to run out • to keep something in mind

Jane Latta

Buying Clothes

CHERYL: Mrs. Filo, I need your help.

MRS. FILO: What do you need, Cheryl? I'll try to help.

CHERYL: Well, in the two years that I've been southwest regional director for my company, I haven't been out of Houston except for a couple of quick trips to New York. Now, the company wants me to represent them in Stockholm at an international convention for two weeks. I have no clothes for that cold climate. Help!

MRS. FILO: Okay, let's not panic. You're going to be gone for two weeks, so you'll need several changes of business-type clothes. No doubt, you'll be attending a few parties and social gatherings while you're there, so you'll want to be able to change from your work clothes into some evening clothes. Am I right?

CHERYL: Yes, I'm sure you are; in fact, there is a rather elegant dinner and dance planned for the last evening of the convention.

MRS. FILO: No problem, Cheryl. I believe we'll be able to outfit you completely. When do you leave?

CHERYL: The conference begins in two weeks. That should be enough time to make any alterations I might need, shouldn't it?

MRS. FILO: Our New Year's rush will be over by then, so I foresee no problems in getting tailoring done. Let's begin with your business suits and dresses. You'll want them warm, of course, but you won't want them to be too much trouble to care for, so all wool is out.

CHERYL: I'd better stick with conservative colors and patterns, Mrs. Filo, and I'd like to coordinate some skirts and blouses so that I can wear the same outfit in several different ways.

MRS. FILO: That's exactly what I had in mind. Here's a smartly tailored darker tweed. It has a soft, casual look, yet it can be worn with a matching jacket which gives it a more professional look. I think you could wear this in any of your meetings, with or without the jacket.

CHERYL: If we add a few blouses and a scarf to pick up the subtle colors in the weave, this one could serve in many capacities. How about something in black too?

MRS. FILO: Perhaps this synthetic blend dress over here. It's warm, yet lightweight. It will travel well, and the best thing is that you can wash it right in your hotel room, hang it up, and it will dry wrinkle-free overnight. This one will come in handy.

CHERYL: I'm so excited about this trip, I can hardly concentrate. Let's go over to the elegant designer gowns. Why are you showing me such somber colors?

MRS. FILO: Don't forget that the climate in Sweden in January is somber. Remember, you don't have to be somber just because you're wearing a dark-colored dress. If you were to wear a bright, summery dress such as the ones women wear here in Texas, you'd look out of place in Sweden.

CHERYL: You're right. I don't want to draw undue attention to myself. Let's see how we can resolve the problem of wanting to look professional and festive at the same time.

MRS. FILO: You still fit into a size 10, don't you?

CHERYL: You're not implying that I'm gaining weight, are you?

MRS. FILO: No. If anything, I was thinking that you had lost weight since I last saw you. We may have to take in the waist and take up the hem of that dark suit you like.

CHERYL: As long as it's ready in time for my trip.

MRS. FILO: I know you didn't come in looking for coats, but I suggest that we also look at winter furs, or at the least, a fur-lined raincoat. It can be awfully cold in Scandinavia at this time of year.

CHERYL: You're right. I may need boots too. I can't believe I'm doing this. I'm buying several new outfits and doubling my wardrobe—all for a two-week trip!

COMPREHENSION AND CONVERSATION PRACTICE

1. Where does this dialogue take place? What people take part in the dialogue?
2. Why is Cheryl in the shop? Where is she going? Why?
3. What kinds of business suits do women wear in your area?
4. What are some examples of *somber* colors? Of *bright* colors?
5. What is the difference between the weather in Houston and the weather in Stockholm?
6. What kind of dress would you (your sister) wear to work? To a party?
7. What is a *designer* gown? Where might you (your sister) wear one?
8. What size dress do you (your sister) wear?
9. How do women's dress sizes differ from those in other countries?
10. Why might a tailor have to *take in* a waist or a shoulder seam?
11. What is your favorite kind of dress material?
12. Describe how Cheryl will wear the same outfit in several different ways.
13. What outfits are in your (your sister's) wardrobe which may be worn in several different ways?
14. What is your (your sister's) favorite dress? What color is it?
15. What alterations were necessary on your (your sister's) favorite dress?

VOCABULARY PRACTICE

1. What date is New Year's Eve?
2. A formal assembly or meeting is called a (convention, shop, business, wardrobe).
3. All the following, except one, are examples of *caring for* one's clothes: washing, buying, dry cleaning, ironing.
4. To be *out of place* means to be (somewhere else, inappropriately dressed, lost, unprofessional).
5. If a store has a New Year's *rush,* it is a time of (inactivity, gaiety, vacation, business).

6. To *resolve a problem* is to (find an answer, ignore it, pose a question, do mathematics).
7. Which of the following is not an item of women's clothing? (blouse, skirt, dress, tailor)
8. Which of the following is a *synthetic* material? (wool, nylon, cotton, silk)
9. A *coordinated outfit* may be called (a frock, a scarf, an ensemble, a coat).
10. To *foresee* is to (remember, anticipate, see four of something, forget).

Use Each of These Phrases in a Sentence

no doubt • out of place • no problem • to care for (something) • to stick with • to have in mind • wrinkle-free • to draw attention (to oneself) • to suit one's needs • to take in (clothing) • as long as

unit (39)

Florida Department of Commerce/Division of Tourism

Taking a Vacation

PHIL: Let's decide where we want to go on vacation this summer.

DON: Are you kidding? Mom and Dad always decide where we're going. They're the ones who pay for it, you know.

PHIL: I know, but if you remember, they always ask us where we want to go. We always say that we don't care or don't know or something like that.

DON: That's because we never believe that they would go where we want to. They always take us where they want to go.

PHIL: Well, let's make it different this year. If you and I decide where we really want to spend two weeks, then we can try to talk them into it.

DON: It's worth a try. Where do you want to go?

PHIL: I liked going to that cabin in the mountains last year. That was fun. Remember all the fun we had going out in the rowboat, and the fishing on the lake?

DON: Yes, but I remember all the mosquitos too. Also, I remember that there weren't any other kids our age to play with. I didn't think it was so much fun.

PHIL: I really loved it. We went rabbit hunting and hiking along the old mountain trails. We picked blueberries. We even learned to ride horses.

DON: All I remember about the horses was the one that threw me off. No. I vote against returning to the mountains. My favorite part of last year's mountain trip was when we stopped at an amusement park on the way home. I loved the roller coaster. My vote goes to the seashore.

PHIL: Do you mean the oceanfront cottage we rented two years ago?

DON: Maybe not the exact same place, but something like it. That was my favorite vacation place of all the places we've gone in the past few years. We were right on the beach where we could go swimming in the ocean or take long walks and collect seashells. It was great.

PHIL: I didn't care for that vacation too much. I remember that I got sunburned the first day we were there, and I had to stay home while everyone chartered that boat to go deep-sea fishing.

DON: That trip was terrific. I remember I caught a small marlin. Don't you remember the fun of building sand castles and playing in the surf? The most fun was meeting all those other kids whose parents had brought them there on vacation. We played volleyball and had beach parties. We even rented bicycles and rode on the boardwalk early in the morning.

PHIL: I remember that I dislike sand. It was everywhere —in my clothes, in the food, in my eyes, in. . . .

DON: You're exaggerating. There must have been something about the shore vacation that you liked.

PHIL: I liked going to that amusement park where there were wild animals that we could see while we drove through the park. The monkeys came up to our car, and we fed them.

DON: That's right, and there was that great roller coaster there too. It was as scary as the one last year!

PHIL: I've got a perfect idea. Let's spend our vacation going to amusement parks!

DON: How can we do it? I mean, how can we talk them into going only to amusement parks?

PHIL: We'll say that we want to go camping. As a matter of fact, we both enjoy camping, so we won't be making it up. We'll get out the map to see where all the great amusement parks are; then we'll trace a route which takes us to as many of them as we can manage. Next, we'll find out where campgrounds are all along that route. When we're finished, we'll show the map to Mom and Dad and tell them we want to camp all along the route.

DON: And if, while we're camping, we happen to notice that there is an amusement park nearby, then. . . .

COMPREHENSION AND CONVERSATION PRACTICE

1. Where does this conversation take place? Is there any way to know?
2. How old do you think Don and Phil are? Which is older?
3. Where did the family go on vacation last year? The year before?
4. Would you enjoy a vacation in the mountains?
5. What are some vacation-type activities in the mountains?
6. What animals do you have in your area?
7. Would you enjoy a vacation at the seashore?
8. What are some vacation-type activities at the seashore?
9. Do you enjoy swimming in the ocean? In a pool? A lake?
10. Would you like to go fishing? Where? For what type of fish?
11. Where are there amusement parks in your area?
12. What is your favorite amusement park ride?
13. Would you enjoy going camping? What is camping like?
14. Where did your parents take you on vacation when you were young?
15. Where would you like to go on vacation this year?

VOCABULARY PRACTICE

1. *Are you kidding* means (Are you young? Do you own goats? Are you serious? Are you angry?).
2. The difference between "I want to go" and "I *really* want to go" is one of (intensity, truth, imagination, reality).
3. A *mosquito* is (a bird, a mammal, a fish, an insect).
4. A *marlin* is a fish found in (the ocean, lakes, streams, rivers).
5. *Deep-sea fishing* takes place (in the ocean, on the beach, in the surf, from the dock).
6. To *charter* a boat is to (buy it, borrow it, rent it, collect it).
7. All of the following, except one, are ways to express the telling of an untruth: make it up, lie, fib, get it out.
8. A *seashell* can come from which of these? (horses, monkeys, clams, marlin)
9. To *hike* is to (swim, ride a bicycle, ride a roller coaster, go on an extended walk).

10. If you don't *care for* something, you don't (tend to it, like it, nurse it, hate it).

Use Each of These Phrases in a Sentence

Are you kidding? • if you remember • to spend (a vacation) • to be worth a try • to play with • to stop at (a place) • to go swimming/ hiking/fishing/camping/horseback riding • to talk someone into (something) • to drive through

Library of Congress

Celebrating Holidays

BEN: Mr. Holmes, I want to ask you a question about American holidays. We don't celebrate Halloween in my country, but everyone tells me that they are going to dress up as ghosts, goblins, witches, or something else on October 31.

MR. HOLMES: That's right, Ben. On that night, children dress up and go door to door asking for treats or playing tricks. The word comes from a shortening of All Hallowed Eve, which means the holy night before the feast of All Saints, November 1.

BEN: Why isn't it a holiday from school? We celebrated Columbus Day, October 12, by taking the day off from school to commemorate the birth of Christopher Columbus.

MR. HOLMES: I guess it's not important or serious enough to give us any time off from school, Ben. We can't take off for every holiday, you know. Besides, we're going to have two days off next month, the Thursday and Friday of Thanksgiving. Does anyone know why we celebrate Thanksgiving?

KIM: I do. It's a festival celebrating the harvest such as they have in many cultures. In the United States, however, it specifically relates to a holiday declared in 1621 after the first harvest by the Pilgrims in their new land.

MR. HOLMES: That's right, Kim. The day has been celebrated since that time. Although the custom lapsed at various times prior to the Civil War, it was officially revived by President Lincoln in 1863. On what day of the year do we celebrate Thanksgiving, and how is it celebrated?

KIM: My family moved here last year, so I learned about it then. Thanksgiving is celebrated on the fourth Thursday in November. There are football games and great big dinners. Most people eat turkey and pumpkin pie and other special dishes.

MR. HOLMES: Right. William, will you please tell us some other holidays which people in the United States celebrate.

WILLIAM: Two that I can think of are Memorial Day and Labor Day.

MR. HOLMES: Good. Memorial Day is celebrated on the thirtieth of May in honor of dead Americans who served in the armed forces. Do you know how it is observed?

WILLIAM: People everywhere visit cemeteries and decorate the graves of dead soldiers with plants and flowers. They also have parades. Labor Day is celebrated on the first Monday of September. It is a day set aside to honor the working people of the United

States and to give them an official day of rest.

MR. HOLMES: That's right. Now, who can tell me why we celebrate the Fourth of July?

SUMIO: The Fourth of July is Independence Day. It was on July 4, 1776 that the Declaration of Independence was signed, proclaiming the independence from England of the thirteen original colonies which later became the United States of America. We celebrate it by going on picnics on that date and going to parades and fireworks displays in the evening.

MR. HOLMES: You've studied your U.S. history well, Sumio. Do you know any of the minor holidays? I call them minor because they are not celebrated as full holidays everywhere throughout the country. In fact, as with Halloween, sometimes all the schools, banks, and businesses remain open as though there were no holiday at all.

SUMIO: Some minor holidays are Lincoln's Birthday, February 12; Washington's Birthday, February 22; Good Friday, a Christian observance on the Friday before Easter Sunday; Yom Kippur, the Jewish day of atonement; Rosh Hashana, Jewish New Year; Martin Luther King's Birthday, January 15; and Veteran's Day, November 11. Two major holidays which we didn't mention are Christmas Day, December 25, and New Year's Day, January 1, but those two are celebrated in many countries around the world.

COMPREHENSION AND CONVERSATION PRACTICE

1. Where does this dialogue take place? What people take part in the dialogue? How many students take part?
2. When is Halloween? How do people celebrate it?
3. When is Thanksgiving? Why do we celebrate it?
4. How did the custom of eating turkey on Thanksgiving begin? What is a turkey?
5. When is Labor Day? Why is it celebrated?
6. When is Memorial Day? Why is it celebrated? How?
7. Why is the Fourth of July a national holiday in the United States?
8. Do people celebrate Independence Day in your country? When is it?
9. What are some other minor holidays in the United States?
10. What are the major and minor holidays in your country?
11. How do you celebrate New Year's Day?
12. Why do schools, banks, businesses, etc., close on holidays?
13. When is the next school holiday?
14. On which holidays do people give gifts?
15. Which is your favorite holiday? Why?

VOCABULARY PRACTICE

1. A *feast* is a (period of fasting, dance, elaborate meal, concert).
2. *Prior to* means (after, before, immediately, during the period of).
3. To *proclaim* is to (announce officially, reduce, insist, desire greatly).
4. The word *bury* rhymes with (carry, fury, cherry, hurry).
5. To *revive* is to (suffocate, drown, penalize, bring back to life).
6. What are the opposites of these words? (minor, similar, close, end, southern, great, present, right, first, quiet)
7. Name the holidays which are celebrated in January, February, and November.
8. What holidays are celebrated on October 12, May 30, and the Friday before Easter?

9. A day on which students and teachers don't have school is called a day (out, about, on, off).
10. Another way of saying *and so forth* is (and so, et cetera, go forth, and).

Use Each of These Phrases in a Sentence

something else • door to door • to take off • to set aside • prior to • to go on a picnic • and so forth • as though

NOTES

NOTES

NOTES

NOTES